T0203492

JavaScript and Open Data

To the memory of Nicolas Classeau, 43, Director of IUT/Marne-la-Vallée,
killed in the Bataclan terrorist attack, November 13, 2015

Series Editor
Jean-Charles Pomerol

JavaScript and Open Data

Robert Jeansoulin

WILEY

First published 2018 in Great Britain and the United States by ISTE Ltd and John Wiley & Sons, Inc.

Apart from any fair dealing for the purposes of research or private study, or criticism or review, as permitted under the Copyright, Designs and Patents Act 1988, this publication may only be reproduced, stored or transmitted, in any form or by any means, with the prior permission in writing of the publishers, or in the case of reprographic reproduction in accordance with the terms and licenses issued by the CLA. Enquiries concerning reproduction outside these terms should be sent to the publishers at the undermentioned address:

ISTE Ltd
27-37 St George's Road
London SW19 4EU
UK

www.iste.co.uk

John Wiley & Sons, Inc.
111 River Street
Hoboken, NJ 07030
USA

www.wiley.com

© ISTE Ltd 2018
The rights of Robert Jeansoulin to be identified as the author of this work have been asserted by him in accordance with the Copyright, Designs and Patents Act 1988.

Library of Congress Control Number: 2018937244

British Library Cataloguing-in-Publication Data
A CIP record for this book is available from the British Library
ISBN 978-1-78630-204-5

Contents

Introduction

I.1. Motivation

Two main facts constituted the motivation for writing this book:

– Broad interest in the JavaScript language: the most used on Earth. It is run hundreds of millions times every day[1]: what web page does not use it?

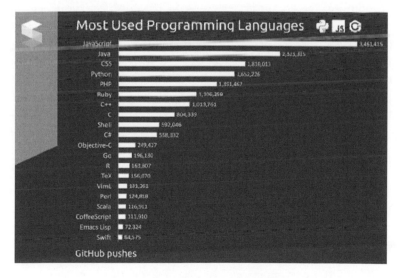

Figure I.1. *Programmers' contributions to the most commonly used computer languages*

1 See https://stackify.com/trendiest-programming-languages-hottest-sought-programming-languages-2017/.

This use ensures regular maintenance of the code and has led to permanent improvement in performance for more than 25 years. In recent years, several innovations of the JavaScript norm have convinced all browser providers to adopt them. Figure I.1., published October 2017, counts the contributions of internauts' coding development in several computer languages.

– Free access to big volumes of data on the Web:

Besides "proprietary" restricted data, public open data (e.g. United Nations, INSEE, US Census Bureau, etc.) [ICS 16] and free access data, via private providers (e.g. shared Google drive) or non-profits (Wikipedia), are an enormous reservoir of universal information.

These two facts have led us to write this book as a JavaScript programming manual, an open data oriented manual, with insight on combining web data and displaying them. Since 2015, the large adoption of recent JavaScript norms encourages their use and greatly facilitates new coding practices, as described in this manual.

Data represent the common heritage of humanity; everyone should have usable and free fetching tools. Every citizen who is curious about data and has a taste for technology may become a "data scientist", an eager amateur, able to study the data, texts or figures of their own focused hobby field. And also in the professional field, a student from a school of political science, or a journalist [NICAR], or the person in charge of an association will find many useful and relevant tools in this book.

I.2. Organization of the book

The sequel of this introduction presents a history of the language for a better understanding of its evolution, a demystification of prejudices, a list of prerequisites and useful tools, and a list of the main features of JavaScript to introduce what the following parts will detail.

– Part 1: This part presents the basics of the language: variables, instructions, tests, string processing, arrays, objects and functions. It also details the specific aspects of JavaScript, its originality in the world of object languages and how it can answer most of the data processing tasks that we highlight in this book. We conclude with some examples of programming by "patterns".

– Part 2: This presents JavaScript in "the ecosystem of the web page", which is composed of the HTTP protocol, the HTML code, the CSS rules and JavaScript as the scripting language. The interface with the elements and events of the HTML DOM ("document object model") allows for the dynamic enrichment of the page on the "client side". Ajax technology allows for the addition of data extracted from the Internet. We address the issues of asynchronous data processing.

– Part 3: This is dedicated to deploying applications:

- accessing open data, free data, combining data from multiple sources by asynchronous "join";

- displaying digital data in graphical plots, animating vector data, cartographic representation;

- creation of JSON files from spreadsheet software, for using JSONP delivery tools, or data directly accessible via different APIs, for converting many data from the Internet into data ready for your applications.

I.3. The history of JavaScript

This historical notice about the birth and life of JavaScript demonstrates another motivation for learning this language: on the computer science scale, it is an "old" language (more 25 years old). How can we explain such longevity? What significant assets allowed such perennity?

– 1993: Release of the web browser Mosaic (which made the World Wide Web popular) by the US NCSA (National Center for Supercomputing Applications).

– 1995: Mosaic becomes Netscape (then: 90% of the market), and asks Brendan Eich to build a scripting language for their Navigator, mimicking Java, released a few months earlier by Sun. Within 2 weeks, the job is done, based upon the language Self (Xerox PARC) and based on "prototypes" instead of "classes" like Java (for respecting the time allowed).

– 1996: Netscape applies JavaScript to the standard body ECMA. Microsoft reacts by developing JScript for Internet Explorer (version 3).

– 2006: W3C specification of the object XMLHttpRequest in order to standardize the use of the Ajax technology on the web.

– 2008: V8, the open source JavaScript engine of Google Chrome.

– 2009: ES5, first version to be adopted in all major browsers.

– 2009: Node.js (Ryan Dahl): JavaScript fully implemented server side.

– 2010: V8 optimized performance competition between browsers.

– 2015: ES6 brings important innovations: "let", "const" declarations, Object.assign method, etc. supported by all the recent browsers.

Year	Name/alias	Description
1998	ECMAScript 2	Editorial changes only
1999	ECMAScript 3/ES3	Added regular expressions, try/catch statement
	ECMAScript 4	*(never released)*
2009	ECMAScript 5/ES5	Added JSON support, Object.create
2015	ECMAScript 6/ES6/ECMAScript2015	Added let, const, Object.assign, arrow syntax, template syntax, spread and rest syntax. Also: classes, modules
2016	ECMAScript 7	Added exponential operator (**), Array#includes

Table I.1. *History of the versions of JavaScript*

I.3.1. *Analyzing this biography of JavaScript*

We can notice several very distinct periods:

– initial success, 1997–1999: evidence of the interest in enriching interactive and dynamic web pages (dynamic HTML, named DHTML);

– stagnation decade, 1999–2009: different versions developed by different browsers, unsuccessful attempts to develop JavaScript on server-side. The design and development of jQuery was the survival response: providing a single access gate to JavaScript ("*code once, run everywhere*");

– revival, 2009: the release of the Ajax technology, the V8 fast compilation, the design of the "off-web" Node.js, the release of the object JSON, all these innovations woke up the JavaScript normalization;

– JavaScript as a generalist language, 2015 to present day: the broad adoption[2] of ES5, then ES6, allows one to overcome many coding pitfalls and performance gains, making the JavaScript engines acceptable even for video and animation.

I.4. To code without "var", nor "for", nor "new"

JavaScript is a lively language, which adapted itself to the evolutions of the new uses of the Internet (e.g. video, social networks, targeted publicity, etc.). More and more web applications massively use JavaScript on the client-side, and even on the server-side, since the release of Node.js and V8.

I.4.1. *Comments*

The foundations of JavaScript are unchanged, but two evolutions deeply modify today's coding practices:

– the majority uses are no longer the same: interactive HTML on the web page has become anecdotal, processing data sources from the Internet via Ajax requests is the big deal;

– recent innovations (ES5, ES6) in the "Core ECMAScript" allow us to better take advantage of the prototypal approach and the functional nature of the language.

I.4.2. *Deliberate bias of this book*

We no longer code JavaScript in 2018 as we did before 2015. Using ES6 allows JavaScript to unleash its qualities rather than its faults:

– Javascript objects are prototype based. Use prototypes and avoid NEW;

– JavaScript functions = first-class objects: code functionally! Avoid "for" loops;

– use the better controlled variable declarations! Ban "var".

And your code will be shorter, more readable, and much, much easier to debug.

---

2 Microsoft turns around the non-compliance of Internet Explorer by releasing Edge.

I.4.3. *Prerequisites*

The Big Data should not be the "preserve of the big actors": everybody with a browser, an Internet connection and some self-training, can work with Big Data. Everybody? As long as they are at least somewhat trained with a few basic notions on:

– the Internet and the World Wide Web (WWW);

– HyperText Markup Language (HTML) and a minimal knowledge of Cascading Style Sheets (CSS);

– the "Developer" tools of any browser (this book's examples are checked with the open-source Firefox).

I.4.4. *Some useful, easy, and free programming tools*

Your browser knows how to interpret JavaScript (it is the training tool) and most of the time without the need for an Internet connection:

– to display the result of some script (see "Part 2"): write a simple web page including that script and use the "Web Console" or "Browser Console".

– the browser "ScratchPad" (checked with Firefox) is useful for quickly testing a few lines of code: it displays `console.log` results and variable values in comments.

Besides, there are several "online tools" for helping us:

– W3Schools: allows both HTML+JavaScript code to be tested, as well as providing a convenient tutorial and most API references;

– JSBin and JSFiddle: these are popular among developers and provide a similar context, in which you can archive more easily;

– Thimble (Mozilla): makes it possible to build cooperative projects if you are coding in a team;

– JSLint: provides online lexical analysis of your JavaScript (see also ESLint).

Most of the code "bins" of this book have been tried with W3Schools.

I.5. Mechanisms and features of the script language

I.5.1. *JavaScript is interpreted and run within an ecosystem*

JavaScript is a scripting language, whose interpretation and execution depend on a script engine that requires a "host", an environment providing basic objects, events and resources.

We must distinguish the "core JavaScript", common foundations of the language, and the embedded JavaScript that includes the objects of a specific environment (e.g. "client-side JavaScript").

Within the "web page ecosystem", the environment is the browser (the "window" object). We may also find the "workers", provided by the browser, but independent of the web page and the ecosystem of the Node.js modules, totally independent of any browser.

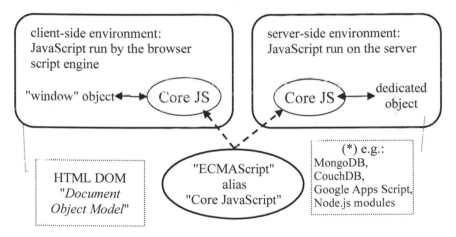

Figure I.2. *JavaScript needs a host environment*

I.5.2. *What does a JavaScript engine do?*

The script engine analyzes then runs the code in the hosting environment, which is named the "Global Object". As soon as the engine starts, it executes two successive tasks:

– the lexical analysis ("lexical-time" or "read-time") and production of a machine bytecode;

– the execution of the machine code ("run-time"). The V8 engine compiles (full-codegen), then optimizes in real time (crankshaft) to improve performance.

From the programmer's viewpoint, this means:

– the lexical declarations are parsed first, and the variable values are initialized to "undefined", whose type is "undefined". Try these lines:

```
let x; // declaration without explicit definition (no assignment)
console.log( x );
console.log( typeof x );
```

– assignments are processed at run-time: definition of variables, typing, evaluation of expressions, etc. whatever appears on the right-hand side of an assignment sign "=".

I.5.3. *Variables and instructions: the functionalities of an "imperative language"*

The lexical analysis lists the variables and their "scope" (where they are known). The run-time defines the variables (gives them a defined value) and also determines their type: the type of value. We may name this "dynamic typing", rather than "weak typing". The values can be: primitive values (numbers, strings, boolean constants), evaluated expressions, references to objects, arrays, functions or regular expressions.

The instructions can be assignments, function calls and classic control structures such as loops or conditional instructions.

I.5.4. *Objects: functionalities of a "prototype-based object-oriented language"*

The objects can be "built-in" (Object, Function, Array, Date, Math, JSON, etc.) or provided by the "host ecosystem", such as the DOM elements (document HTML), or built by the application.

JavaScript makes no distinction between "class" and "instance" notions: there are only objects and any object may become the "prototype" used to create new objects. We may wrap-up the definition of a JavaScript object as "a set of properties plus one prototype".

I.5.5. *Functions as "first-class objects": the functionalities of a "functional language"*

Functions and objects behave in the same way, except that only a function can be invoked, or called. Any operation supported by an object is supported by a function: it makes it possible to build a "higher order function" and grounds the functional nature of JavaScript:

```
const mult = function(f,g){return function(n){return f(n)*g(n);}},
    square = function(x) { return x * x; };
mult(square, square)(3);    // -> 81
```

I.6. Conclusion

JavaScript is born for the web, and because of the web, JavaScript still lives 25 years later, and this is the motivation for writing this book. A small language, designed within 2 weeks by only one person, has proven to be surprisingly flexible. This flexibility is both an advantage, which allowed evolution and compliance with successive versions, and a drawback, in that it does not protect enough against programming errors, hard to detect and debug. JavaScript has been qualified as the "most misunderstood language" from one of its main "gurus", Doug Crockford.

A tolerance that is too big, a control that is too weak, no "classes" for the objects, a syntax much too similar to the style of imperative and procedural languages; here are many deceptive pitfalls. By contrast, the initial choice of functions as "first-class objects" gives JavaScript the abilities of a functional language: a skill that is neglected by many programmers.

Recent normalization efforts provide new ways to avoid most pitfalls: we can code without var declaration (avoiding many "hoisting" traps), without for loops (avoiding index troubles), and almost without the "new" operator (for a more direct use of prototypes). This leads to writing a more readable and easier-to-debug code.

The surprising book "*If Hemingway wrote JavaScript*" (see [CRO 14]) shows how it is possible to render unrecognizable, and in several different ways, a JavaScript code that, nevertheless, always carries out the same operation.

Core JavaScript

Introduction to Part 1

This part deals with the fundamentals of JavaScript, whatever the environment in which it is hosted. Most of the time, JavaScript is associated with a browser, but it is a language by itself. We use the term "Core JavaScript" or "ECMAScript" to mean what is "pure JavaScipt", in contrast with what is added by the environment into which JavaScript is embedded.

There is no need to be a JavaScript expert, good applications can be quickly programmed, provided that you adopt some "good practices". Coding without good practice (aka. "anti-pattern") may seem correct while being silently error prone, with errors difficult to spot. That is why you will find "Recommendations" paragraphs throughout the chapters, suggesting ways to encode "patterns". ES5 and ES6 standards facilitate this type of coding.

Part 1 can be used as a manual: going directly to the section that concerns one immediate problem, or instead studying a chapter more in depth, for instance with the sensitive issues of the language (e.g. prototypes, closures). Here is a quick tour of the features of this amazing language:

– Variables: declaration, definition, types (ban every "`var`"):

Here, we insist on the subtle distinction between the status of "declared" and "defined" variables, which deserves a particular attention. In this chapter, the creation of the tree structure of "variable scopes", the implicit "hoisting" and the (dangerous) implicit declaration of global variables are presented. The ES6 version provides new declaration keywords, which can avoid many (silent) causes of error.

– Controls: booleans, tests and loops (replace "for" loops by array methods):

JavaScript looks classically procedural, when it comes to controlling the status of variables. But several operators may react surprisingly, due to their "polymorphism": they do not react in the same way according to the type (e.g. number or string) and implicit (silent) recasting can be done. We emphasize such traps, and suggestions are provided to avoid them.

– Data: characters used as numbers, and strings and dates:

An appropriate format is required to represent quantitative (numbers) or qualitative data (names, texts, dates). Any unicode character can be used, and figures can be used within numbers or names or dates: we detail some issues related to type conversions and value comparisons, which are among the tricky points.

– Objects (restrict "new" to built-in or APIs objects):

The construction of specific objects is required to structure linked data into meaningful information and to assign it the appropriate methods. The objects in JavaScript are treated rather differently than in most object-oriented languages. We focus on the innovations of ES6 that provide better tools to build objects in the "prototype" way.

– Arrays (get rid of loops "for"):

To handle time series or relational data, tables and matrices are required. We detail the most useful methods, added to the JavaScript Array object since ES5 or ES6, that make it possible to avoid the loops, rewriting them in a "functional" code style.

– Functions (do program functionally, as often as possible):

Functions are "first-class objects" in JavaScript. This is probably the most important part of this language, and the key reasons for its efficiency and longevity.

Variables: Declaration, Definition and Type

Variables are made to receive values directly or through evaluated expressions compounding values and operators or results of function calls: the value is stored internally and the variable references this storage, and takes its value and its type.

There are two kinds of values:

– primitive values: numbers or strings in literal notation, "built-in" values such as true, false, NaN, infinity, null, undefined, etc.;

– objects, including functions, and arrays, which are "containers", and, as such, their value is the address of the container.

NOTE.– The content of a container can be modified, while the address remains unchanged (this is important for understanding the "const" declaration below).

To fetch the value of a variable, it must have been identified in the lexical phase: which means to be "declared". Often, JavaScript code starts with declaration instructions such as:

```
var tableauCandidats = [];
var n = 0; // ... ...
```

We will show why it is highly preferable to write:

```
const tableauCandidats = [];
let n = 0; // ... ...
```

Let us look back at the two steps in the interpretation of JavaScript (simplified):

– Lexical-time: It deals with the lexical analysis of the code. The names of the declared functions and variables are recorded in a tree structure (lexical tree). Declarations are moved up to the beginning of their block of code: this is named the "hoisting". Functions are hoisted first, for they define the nodes of the structure, then variables are attached to appropriate nodes.

– Run-time: The script engine reads the instructions again and runs them one by one, with the help of the tree structure. Expressions (right-hand side of assignment instructions) are evaluated, and values are assigned to variables (on the left-hand side) with the associated type (dynamic typing).

Let us detail this double mechanism: declaration of the variables, initialization to undefined at *lexical-time* and definition of the variables at *run-time*.

1.1. Declarations of functions and variables

For a better understanding of the declaration mechanism in JavaScript, we must first learn what the "scope" of a variable is: the function declarations determine the overall logics of the notion of scope.

1.1.1. *The different declaration keywords*

1.1.1.1. *Function declaration*

The keyword comes first in the instruction line; the syntax is:

```
function name (list, of, parameters) { block_of_code }
```

At lexical time, the name is stored in the lexical tree as a new function node. The list of parameters, and all variables and functions declared within the block, are added to this node. New declared functions open new nodes as subnodes: this is a recursive process (depth-first analysis). We will detail this in Chapter 6, section 6.4.1.1.

Therefore, every function determines a "function scope". At the beginning of the lexical analysis, the engine uses a "root node" that is named the "global scope".

NOTES.–

1) A variable that does not appear in the lexical tree (i.e., never declared) cannot be assigned to another variable; for its evaluation, it is impossible: a Reference Error is triggered.

2) An attempt to assign a (evaluable) value to a never declared variable, for instance, x = 1 with x absent from the lexical tree, is not an error. Therefore, the variable is added to the global scope. This is bad practice, an "anti-pattern" (see case [f4]).

1.1.1.2. *var declaration*

Before 2015, the only way to declare a variable was the old-fashioned declaration keyword, which can be used in one of these forms:

```
var x;                              // simple declaration
var x = [[val]];                    // declaration with definition
var x = [[val]], y = [[val]], z;    // multiple declarations
```

The declaration is hoisted at the beginning of the function scope or the global scope. The variable, if not explicitly defined with a value, receives the value undefined. That value is hoisted together with the reference.

NOTE. If JavaScript is embedded in a browser, the "global scope" is the window object:

```
var a; // equivalent: 'window.a' (a as a property of window)
function f(){var a;} // this 'a' is different from 'window.a'
```

1.1.1.3. *let declaration*

The keyword let acts as var, and moreover limits the scope of the variable to the context of a block: for instance, a conditional instruction block, a function block or the global scope.

There is another difference: no "hoisting" is applied to the variable, hence there is a gap between the lexical existence (whole block) and the existence of the reference (declaration line). This means that, during that gap, any attempt to fetch that reference will trigger an error:

```
{ /* new block */
  console.log(x);
```

```
// ReferenceError: can't access lexical declaration x before initialization
  let x = 4;
}
```

And there is an additional constraint: it is forbidden to redeclare the same name in the same block:

```
let x = 1; let x = 2;   // SyntaxError: redeclaration of let x
let x = 1; x = 2;       // the redefinition is allowed
```

These constraints provide a better protection against unwilling modifications of the lexical context.

1.1.1.4. *const declaration*

In this, the keyword behaves like let with two additional constraints:

– declaration AND definition must be done in the same instruction, and any redeclaration is forbidden:

```
const Euler; // SyntaxError: missing = in const declaration
```

– redefinition is forbidden:

```
const Pi = 3.14; // the value of Pi est defined only once
Pi = 3.1; // TypeError: invalid assignment to const `PI'
```

– redeclaration with the same or a different keyword is equally forbidden:

```
const pi = 3; let pi = 3; // SyntaxError: redeclaration of const
function y(){}
let y; // SyntaxError: redeclaration of function y
```

Note about const: A variable already defined cannot be redefined, which means that if the value is an object, you will always use the same object, as a container, but its properties can be modified as often as you need.

Therefore, the use of const is highly recommended for objects, arrays and function's expressions.

Note about the three keywords: var is the most "permissive", hence the most error prone; const is the most constraining, hence detects the greatest number of coding inconsistencies, right at the lexical stage:

The recommendation is to privilege const, unless you know that the variable is used temporarily, and will evolve soon. For instance, an index, a cumulative value, a boolean control, etc.

1.1.2. Lexical scope and definition of a variable according to declaration mode: `var, let, const`

Let us present some examples to illustrate the differences between pre-ES6 and post-ES6 situations, depending on four different cases. In all the following cases, we assume that the variable x is never declared elsewhere in the global scope.

1.1.2.1. Situation pre-ES6

Here are four functions, corresponding to four cases. In Tables 1.1 and 1.2, we fetch the type and value of x, within or outside the function, and before and after the declaration instruction. The use of var shows how "permissive" and risky it is.

Pre-ES6. Four cases for a variable in a function scope (or not)	

`// f1: no declaration, no definition of 'x'`
`function f1() { /* no occurrence of x in function */ }`
`// f2: declaration of 'x' but no definition`
`function f2() { /* local before */ var x;    /* local after */ }`
`// f3: declaration an definition in the same instruction,`
`function f3() { /* local before */ var x = 1; /* local after */ }`
`// f4: assignation of a value to 'x' without declaration.`
`function f4() { /* local before */ x = 1;    /* local after */ }`	

f1 Local	{ type: undefined}, val -> *ReferenceError: x is not defined*
global before call	{ type: undefined}, val -> *ReferenceError: x is not defined*
global after	{ type: undefined}, val -> *ReferenceError: x is not defined*
f2 local, before var	{ type: undefined, val: undefined};
after var	{ type: undefined, val: undefined };
global after	{ type: undefined}, val -> *ReferenceError: x is not defined*

f3 local, before var	{ type: undefined, val: undefined },
after var	{ type: number, val: 1 };
global after	{ type: undefined}, val -> *ReferenceError: x is not defined*
f4 local, before =	{ type: undefined}, val -> *ReferenceError: x is not defined*
after =	{ type: number, val: 1 };
global after	{ type: number, val: 1 }; // !!! beware !!!

Table 1.1. *Lexical scope and value of a variable (four cases), using var declaration*

COMMENTS.–

[f1]: any attempt to fetch the variable always results in type undefined (the operator typeof never throws an error) and a "Reference Error".

[f2]: type and value are "undefined" inside, no reference outside;

[f3]: type and value are updated: "undefined" -> "number", no reference outside;

[f4]: *the most weird and dangerous*: at run-time, the instruction x = 1 does not find any lexical reference for *x*, and the JavaScript engine creates one in the global space. Silently! Which may result in later troubles.

NOTE.– A very frequent and unwilling cause for [f4] is when using loop index: for(i = 0; i <length; i++) { /* code */ }   // DANGER!   Use 'let i' or -better-, try to avoid the loop (Chapter 5).

1.1.2.2. *Situation post-ES6*

Now, let us use let or const, wherever var was used. There is no difference where var was not used, hence, this is not repeated here, and the case f4 is not changed either.

Post-ES6. Different cases for a variable in a function scope (or not)
| ```
function f5() { /*local before*/ let x;       /*local after*/ }
function f6() { /*local before*/ let x = 1;   /*local after*/ }
function f7() { /*local before*/ const x = "Man"; /*local after*/ }
/* f8 would be strictly identical to f4 */
``` |
```

f5	local before	{ type: undefined} -> *ReferenceError: can't access lexical declaration before initialization*
	after	{ type: undefined, val: undefined};
f6	local before	{ type: undefined} -> *ReferenceError: can't access lexical declaration before initialization*
	after	{ type: undefined, val: 1};
f7	local before	{ type: undefined} -> *ReferenceError: can't access lexical declaration before initialization*
	after	{ type: string, val: "Man" }; mandatory
all	cases: global	{ type: undefined} -> *ReferenceError: x is not defined*

Table 1.2. *Lexical scope and value of a variable using let or const declaration*

1.1.3. *Comments (important improvements carried over by ES6)*

Cases [f5] and [f6] are the equivalent of [f2] and [f3]: The difference with let is that we cannot use the variable before its declaration. The text of the error tells us that the problem resides *within the block*; if outside, the message would be: *ReferenceError: x is not defined*. This is very useful for tracking bugs.

When using const, the only possible case is [f7], equivalent of [f3]: if you forget to assign a value, the error is: *SyntaxError: missing = in const declaration*.

1.1.4. *General conclusion about the variable declarations in JavaScript*

Considering the four possible cases with declarations:

– const is the most constraining, leading to less risky situations: limited lexical scope, no redeclaration, no redefinition and clearer messages. Moreover, the declaration and the definition are necessarily done by a single instruction line, which results in (a) more readable code and (b) immutable type. An immutable type is better for helping the script engine to optimize its bytecode, resulting in better performance.

– var is the most permissive, hence the most risky: unwilling redeclarations are a frequent cause of silent error. In this, a keyword exists for legacy reasons; you must ban it from your code.

– let should be used in the cases where you intend to reuse the same variable name: incrementing a number, or modifying a string, or a boolean constant. For referencing containers (Objects, Arrays, Functions), use const (see the following chapters). For strings or numbers that are not supposed to change, use const as well.

– absence of declaration: when a variable appears, for the first time, on the left-hand side of an assignment instruction, without a declaration keyword, an implicit declaration is done. It is a programming design mistake, but does not cause a problem for JavaScript. See next sub-section "implicit addition".

Figure 1.1 shows the mechanism of the interpretation of the script, when using the recommended keywords const and let, for x and y, and with a forgotten keyword before z.

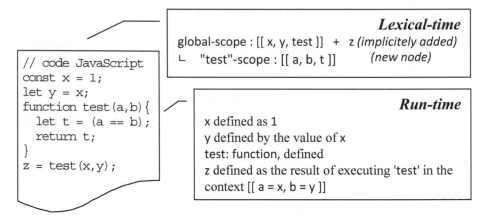

Figure 1.1. *The two phases of the interpretation mechanism*

NOTE 1.– One advantage of using const, if you forget to declare a variable:

```
const Pi = 3.14;        // global: can't be redefined
function calcul(x) {
    Pi = 3.1416;        // a future new global at run-time
    return 2*Pi * x;
}
calcul(2); //TypeError: invalid assignment to const
```

NOTE 2.– If a variable cannot be declared with const because you must modify it, you can embed this variable as a property of an object (see

Chapter 4) and declare that object with const: you will benefit from the advantage of Note 1:

```
const xObj = { x = 3 }; // global: can't be redefine
function calcul(x){
    xObj.x = x; // you can modify the property xObj, but
    xObj = x; // will provoque an error at run-time
}
calcul(2); //TypeError: invalid assignment to const
```

1.1.4.1. *The implicit addition of a variable in the "global scope" (at run-time)*

We have seen that an instruction $x = [[val]]$ may result in an implicit declaration in global scope, if the variable is not present in the lexical tree.

The instruction is ignored at lexical time, and no "hoisting" is made, but at run-time, the name x, on the left-hand side of a valid assignment instruction, is not found in the lexical tree: hence x is added to the global scope.

Note that an instruction $x = x+1$ that would have thrown a "ReferenceError: x is not defined" for the evaluation of the right-hand side is impossible.

1.1.4.2. *Wrapping it up*

The reasons to ban var are as follows:

Var	Let

Redeclaration is possible: YES
var k = 10;
var k = "dix"; // allowed
	Redeclaration: NO
	let k = "dix";
	let k = 10; // Error!

Limitated to a block: NO
// i EXISTS before = undefined
for(var i = 0; i < 5; i++) {
    /* i ok in the loop */ }
// i EXISTS after = 5
	Limitated to a block: YES
	//Error! attempt using i before
	for(let i = 0; i < 5; i++) {
	    /* i ok in the loop */ }
	//Error! if using i after

Hoisting: YES
// n HOISTED = undefined
console.log(n); // undefined
var n = 12;   // = 12
	Hoisting: NO
	// n doesn't exist
	console.log(n); // Error!
	let n = 12; //statement dropped

Table 1.3. *The different behavior of var and let or const*

1.1.5. *Naming variables and functions: best practices*

1) Do not use "reserved words" (see Chapter 7) for it is forbidden. For instance, `function class(c){return "color:"+c;}` will throw a Syntax error because `class` is a reserved word.

2) Never use the same name in two declarations. Using `const` and `let` only protects you from doing so, but several function declarations will not fail: the last one prevails, which may cause damage elsewhere in the code, which is hard to debug.

3) Use good naming practices to facilitate reading of your code:

- avoid meaningless names, except for short-term, buffer-like variables in short blocks of code (typically less than 10 lines of code);

- use "camelCase" notation: it splits words, while avoiding the space ("camel case") or dash ("camel-case") which would be misinterpretated;

- use upper case initial letters only for functions that you intend to use as object constructor (e.g. `let d = new Date();`);

- a constant value can be named in full upper case: `const FRANC = 6.56;`

4) Limit the number of global variables to a minimum, possibly to 1:

REASON.– The JavaScript engine requires an environment, the Global Object. In the environment of the browser, the global object is `window`, an already very "crowdy" object. Every new variable AND function, created in the code, and which is not included in the block of code of a function, ends up in the global object:

```
/* code at the global level */        /* equivalent to */
function f(){   /*local code*/         window.f = function(){ ... };
}                                      window.g = function(){ ... };
function g(){   /*local code*/         window.obj1 = ...
}                                      window.tabInitial = ...
const obj1 = {"a", "b", "c"};
const tabInitial = [];
```

And the window becomes more and more crowded, which is a real performance issue. The solution includes all the code in a single function. This practice is called "the local function".

1.2. Variable definition, initialization and typing in JavaScript

1.2.1. *Variables initialization and definition*

The let-declared variables are defined at run-time, when they appear on the left-hand side of an assignment. Between their declaration (let) and the assignment (=), their value is undefined.

```
let x, y;              // x and y lexically declared.
x = 1;          // x is assigned the value 1
y = x;          // y is assigned the value of x, hence 1
       // or, in a different order
let x, y;              // x and y lexically declared
y = x;          // y is assigned the value of x, hence 'undefined'
x = 1;          // x is assigned the value 1
```

The const-declared variables are declared and initialized just once, avoiding most of these subtleties: use const as often as possible.

If you cannot use const, at least use let in a combined declaration and definition instruction, and preferably at the beginning of the block: this will avoid the definition gap. And this is good for the script engine: the sooner it knows the type, the sooner the bytecode optimization can be applied.

1.2.2. *Types*

We can fetch the type of any variable, thanks to the operator typeof.

A function receives the type "function". For any other variable, the value and the type are determined, at run-time, when the first assignment instruction is met for that variable. With a const declaration, definition and type come at the same time, which is the best situation for code robustness and performance considerations.

With let, we would rather combine declaration and definition:

```
let x; console.log(x +", "+ typeof x); // undefined, undefined
x = 4;                          // only now: 4, number
let y = "4"; console.log(y +", "+ typeof y);    // 4, string
let v = (x>3); console.log(v +", "+ typeof v); // true, boolean
```

In other cases that should be avoided, namely var and "implicitly defined" variables, the value and the type are set by default to "undefined".

Actually this is a "*dynamic typing*", because variables always have a type, which can be "undefined", and the initial type can be modified, except with const. Another reason for using const in priority.

Values in JavaScript are either "primitives" or objects:

– a *primitive* value has no property nor method (see note below): these are built-in values (undefined, null, true, false, NaN), numbers, or strings;

– an object is a collection of named values, couples: {name:value}.

There are six types in JavaScript:

– Type for the undefined variables: "undefined" (valeur undefined)

– Type: boolean   (possible values: true or false)

– Type: number   (e.g. 42, 3.14159, 0x0F, Infinity, NaN)

– Type: string   (e.g. "JavaScript" or "" for the empty string)

– Type: function   const f = function(){}; // typeof: "function"

– Type: object, for any object that is not a function, and includes null.

```
const obj = {"nom": "X", "age": 23};  // typeof obj -> object
```

There are many built-in objects in JavaScript, which all receive the type "object": Object, Array, String, Number, Boolean, Date, RegExp, Error, Math, JSON. The exception is the object Function, whose type is "function". There also exists the object null that makes it possible to initialize explicitly a variable that is unknown (and empty) and could presumably be set later.

NOTE.– There exist objects, Number and String, whose only role is to "bind" the corresponding types "number" and "string" in order to provide their values with appropriate methods. For similar reasons, there exist Array, Function and Object.

You should avoid creating such objects, in particular for primitive values, and rather use their literal notations which we will learn in each respective chapter.

1.2.3. *How to use the type "undefined" and the value undefined*

Never explicitly assign the value undefined to define a variable, though it is allowed. The reason for not using undefined, together with other previous recommendations, is:

a) a variable declared with const cannot be undefined;

b) a variable declared with let with an assignment, is not undefined.

Hence, a variable with an undefined value comes from an "implicit declaration", which is easier to determine, by checking:

```
if(typeof x === 'undefined'){ alert("declaration is missing"); }.
```

In situations where it is impossible to define a variable at the time of the declaration, we use:

```
let x = null;
```

2

Controls: Booleans, Branch and Loops

2.1. Truth values and boolean operators

A control is a *boolean context* that is defined by the syntax of a conditional instruction:

– branch: if(exp. in boolean context) {evaluated true} else {evaluated false};

loop: while (exp in boolean context) {repeat block of code}.

As is no surprise, there are two boolean values: true and false. What is more specific is that, in a *boolean context*, the values of type string or number are cast to a boolean, and values undefined and null are evaluated as false.

2.1.1. *Boolean operators: "!" (not), "&&" (and), " ||" (or)*

Allowing to build logical expressions in classical boolean logics, we get:

```
let p = true, q = false;
console.log( typeof p);     // -> boolean
console.log( p || q);          // -> disjonction -> true
console.log( !p || q);      // -> logical imply: p => q () -> false
```

NOTE.– Evaluation from left to right, priority to inner parentheses, short-cut rules.

```
let bool1 = true, bool2 = false;
let p = bool1 || bool2; // bool2 not evaluated: p already 'true'
let q = bool2 && bool1; // bool1 not evaluated; q already 'false'
```

2.1.2. Relational operators: >, <, >=, <=

With numbers, the relation is the order relation in $\Re$ (real numbers); with strings, it is the Unicode order relation where figures [0-9] precede alphas.

```
let x = 4; console.log(x>3); console.log(x>'3'); // 'true' 'true'
console.log('b' > 'a'); console.log('b' > '3'); // 'true' 'true'
// warning! figures are like characters, hence:
console.log('20'>'2'); console.log('20'>'3'); // 'true' 'false' !
```

WARNING.– When reading external data sources (e.g. JSON file), figures can be cast as numbers or as strings. You should inspect how it is actually done: this is a frequent cause of error (see Part 3).

2.1.3. Comparison operators: ==, != (simple) or ===, !== (strict)

There exist two versions of the comparison operator.

2.1.3.1. Simple equality (==), resp. inequality (!=)

The type of the operands is checked first:

– if different, a prior type conversion is performed;

– result is 'true' if the operands values are equal (respectively, inequal)

2.1.3.2. Strict equality (===), respectively inequality (!==)

The type of the operands is checked first:

– if different, the result is 'false' (respectively, 'true');

– else, result is 'true' if operands values are equal (respectively, inequal).

By construction, the strict equality can return earlier (best performance). Example of differences is as follows:

```
let x=4; console.log(x == 4); console.log(x == '4');
              // 'true'              'true'
```

```
console.log(x === 4); console.log(x === '4');
          // 'true'                  'false'
```

Recommendation: Use the "strict comparison" operators.

NOTE.– In boolean context, all the following values, with their type in parentheses, are cast to false: undefined ("undefined"), null ("object"), 0 ("number"), NaN ("number"), "" ("string") → false ("boolean").

2.2. Conditional instructions: branch test, loop test

2.2.1. *Conditional instructions: if ... else, if ... else if ... else*

The following example ends up printing "a equals 0":

```
let a = 0, str = "";
if (a !== undefined)    // if (a): try it instead
  {
    if (a < 0) {
        str = 'a is strictly negative';
    } else if (a > 0) {
        str = 'a is strictly positive';
    } else {
        str = 'a equals zero';
    }
} else {str = 'a is undefined';}
console.log(str);      // 'a equals zero'
```

NOTE.– By using if(a) instead of if(a !== "undefined"), the value 0 is cast to false and you get 'a is undefined'.

2.2.2. *Ternary conditional operator*

The same example can be written with two nested ternary operators (.. ? .. : ..):

```
let a = 0, str = "";
str = a === undefined ? 'a is undefined':
          ( a > 0? 'a is strictly positive':
              ( a < 0? 'a is strictly negative': 'a equals zero'));
```

2.2.3. *Instruction "switch"*

If you have to choose between possible values of one variable, a convenient and readable way is the switch instruction. Note, in the example, how the presence/absence of break affects the result:

```
let a = 'w', b = 0, c = 0;
switch (a) {
    case 'y':
        c++; break; // terminates the switch
    case 'w':
        b++; c++;
        // no break here: continue with next instruction: b++; //see:
warning
    case 'x':
        b++; break;  // terminates the switch
    default: // always end a switch with a default, even empty
        b = false; // break is useless after the last instruction
}
console.log(a +' => '+ b +', '+ c); // -> w => 2, 1
```

Warning! The absence of a break in a switch is bad practice, because modifying one case may unwillingly modify the preceding case, and it is rather difficult to track such bugs. Always use break.

2.2.4. *Classical iteration loop: instruction "for"*

The general syntax is provided by this example:

```
for (let i = 0; i < 4; i++) { /* i -> successively: 0 ... 3 */ }
```

For several reasons, we have warned against using var. With the index of the loop, using var means that the value of i is undefined (default), or any value, before entering the loop, and equal to the maximum value plus one (4 in the example), after leaving the loop. This is bad practice to rely on such a variable. Inversely, using let ensures that the index does not exist outside of the loop. If the same name i is used, it is a different and independent variable.

A frequent problem is the omission to declare the index: it becomes a global variable and can be modified from anywhere: this is a frequent cause of error:

```
for ( i = 0; i < 4; i++) { /* i -> successively: 0 ... 3 */ }
```

Use let to declare the index, or, better, avoid using loops.

2.2.5. Repeat under condition: instructions "while", and "do..while"

Syntax of the while:

```
while ( test ) { /* code run if and until test is 'true' */
}
```

and syntax of the do..while:

```
do {  /* code is run once, then until test is 'true' */
} while ( test )
```

The difference is that do executes the code at least once.

NOTE.– In Chapter 4, we will learn the instruction for..in, which, in spite of a similar name, is very different from the for loop, for it is a simple enumerator of the properties of an object (no test, no index).

2.2.6. Implicit casting of values "undefined" and "null" in boolean context

The value undefined is characteristic of a never defined variable. The type "undefined" applies to a never defined variable and to a never declared variable.

We can play with either one to build appropriate tests:

```
if (typeof foo === 'undefined') {
    // runs if 'foo' is not defined OR doesn't exist (not declared)
    // no error thrown: always proceed.
}
if (foo === undefined) {
    // runs if 'foo' is not defined. ReferenceError if not declared
}
if (foo === null) {
    // runs if 'foo' is defined as 'null', and its type is 'object'
    // ReferenceError if not declared
}
```

```
if(!foo) {
    // covers cases: undefined, null, 0, NaN, "", false
    // ReferenceError if not declared
}
```

NOTE.– In a "numerical context" (see Chapter 3), the implicit conversions of the values `undefined` and `null` give different results, respectively `NaN` and `0`:

```
let a; let x = a+2;          // x -> NaN
let a = null; let x = a+2;   // x -> 2
```

In this particular situation, it may be better to have an error rather than letting the code continue silently with an incorrect numerical value.

If you need to initialize a variable of an unknown type and with an unknown value, use "null".

2.2.7. Short-cut evaluation: tips for the uncertain definitions

The operators `&&` and `||` are evaluated with the shortcut rule: the next operand is evaluated depending on the status of the test after the previous operand evaluation. It can help in shortening the code in situations such as:

– checking if an object is not `null` before fetching one of its properties:

```
let name = ob && ob.getName(); // avoids an error
// if ob is 'null', ob.getName() will not be invoked
```

– initializing a variable with a valid value OR with a default value:

```
let name = str || "default name";
// if str is "" (empty string, uses "default name" instead
```

2.2.8. Exception handling

We have met several situations, during lexical time or run-time, where controls are impossible, due to the non-existence of a variable or a function, for instance when a variable has never been declared. These kinds of errors, `ReferenceError`, `SyntaxError` ... are named "exceptions".

The `typeof` operator will always work, but it is of a limited use. There is a better way to deal with exceptions and to allow a code to terminate cleanly.

The instruction is try..catch..finally. We can also send our own exception with the instruction throw and combine both instructions. Here is an example:

```
let done = false, someData = "";
openDataBase();          // for instance: open a data flow
try {
    let result = process(someData);
    if (!result) {       // throw an exception
            throw new Error("unlucky!");
    }
} catch (e) {            // catch any exception thrown
        console.log(e.name + ": " + e.message);
} finally {              //  [optional] instructions always run
        done = true;
        closeDataBase();     // close the data flow in all cases
}
```

Any object can be used with throw, but we should rather use the built-in Error or one variant. The object Error is thrown if an error occurs during the lexical analysis, or during the execution, or from a built-in method during run-time.

Variant	Description
EvalError	Error during the evaluation (e.g. implicit conversion)
InternalError	Error thrown by the engine (e.g. "too much recursion")
RangeError	Error when the number is outside its valid range
ReferenceError	Search for a variable from an invalid reference
SyntaxError	Syntax error during lexical analysis
TypeError	Error when the type of a variable is wrong
URIError	Error with invalid parameters to encodeURI() / decode

Table 2.1. *Different variants of the Error object*

More errors can be thrown by an external API, such as the HTMLDOM DOMError from the web page, or by an Ajax request.

2.2.8.1. *Checking a bunch of features in a single block*

If there are several features in part of the code, which may depend on external resources, or which are not necessarily implemented in a particular browser environment, it could be easier to check all of them at once, with a sequence try..catch..finally rather than checking every one individually.

```
let htm = "";
try {
    const x = new window.Date();
    const y = new window.webWorker();
    const z = new XMLHttpRequest();
}
catch(e){
    const s = "!Try: "+e.message; htm += "<br>"+s;
    throw new Error(s);}
finally{
    htm += "<br>job completed";
    console.log(htm); // display htm in ".log"
  }
}
```

We can check more precisely among several exception variants:

```
try { foo.bar(); }
catch (e) {     // check which sub-kind of Error
        if (RangeError.isPrototypeOf(e)) {
                console.log(e.name + " data: " + e.message); }
        else if (URIError.isPrototypeOf(e)) {
                console.log(e.name + " network: " + e.message); }
        // ... etc
}
```

The instruction catch exists also with the Promise object (see Chapter 10).

3

Data: Numbers and Strings

Developing and mastering the natural language has brought humankind a decisive advantage on our planet. Interpreting sounds or written signs is the first step. For a computer, this interpretation is not as soft and flexible as it is for human beings. In any real application, the first obstacle when reading a number or a piece of text is to correctly include it into the processing flow.

A single sign may mean different things: figures 7 and 10 can be numbers, but in "Ronaldo wears the 7, and Maradona the 10", it is just nonsense to add 7 and 10.

Different words may mean the same thing: "Général De Gaulle" and "Charles de Gaulle", or simply "Jean Pierre" and "Jean-Pierre".

An illustration is given with the electoral data in Part 3: the difficulties in identifying a same single candidate when the name can be differently written out in two different files.

In this chapter, we visit "numbers" and "strings", and in particular the use of:

– concatenation operator (+), and comparisons with type string variables;

– methods of the object String and String.prototype;

– regular expressions and the object RegExp.

3.1. Handling numbers

3.1.1. *Literal notation of type "number" variables*

The literal notation of numbers can take several forms:

```
4.2            encodes the real number 4.2
-3e-5          encodes -0.00003 (scientific notation)
0x0f           encodes 15 (hexadecimal notation)
0x0g           SyntaxError: identifier starts immediately after numeric
               literal
               // only characters [0-9, a-f] are allowed after
               prefix 0x0
```

There are two built-in values whose typeof is "number": NaN, Infinity[1].

Evaluation	Result	Type
x = -0x0f / -3e2;	0.05	Number
x = 12 / -0;	-Infinity	Number
x = -100000 * Infinity;	Infinity	Number
x = Infinity / Infinity;	NaN	Number

Table 3.1. *Examples of numeric expression evaluations*

NOTE.– How to know if a value is a number? The value NaN is of type "number", therefore, it is not enough to check if a variable is really different from any number:

```
let t = "", x = 12/0; x = 2*x / x;
if(typeof x !== "number"){t = x +" is not a number";}
else {t = x +" is ok";}
                      // NaN is ok (misleading answer!)
```

The built-in method isNan() returns true for any value that is not a number, including NaN.

```
if(isNaN(x)){t = x +" is really not a number";}
else {t = x +" is really ok";}
                      // NaN is really not a number
```

---

1 Any value above 1.797693135E+308 is evaluated to Infinity (or -Infinity if negative).

3.1.2. *Arithmetic operators*

– *Classical 4 arithmetic operators:* +, -, *, /

```
let x = (20 +5) * 4 / 100; // -> 1
```

It looks classical but with the operator +, if one operand is a "string" (see next), the left to right evaluation will be modified (with respect to the parentheses).

– *Modulo operator:* %

```
let x = 20 % 3; // -> 2
```

– *Exponentiation operator:* **(*any number as exponent, since 2016*)

```
let x = 2 ** (1/2); // -> √2 : 1.4142135623730951
```

WARNING.– Beware of parentheses (suggestion: be explicit).

```
2 ** 3 ** 2          // 512:
2 ** (3 ** 2)        // 512
(2 ** 3) ** 2        // 64
(-2) ** 2            // 4
-2 ** 2              // Syntax Error
-(2 ** 2)            // -4
```

– *Incrementation/decrementation operators (unary):* ++, –

– // Postfix use

```
let x = 3, y = x++; // y = 3, x = 4
```

– // Prefix use

```
let a = 2, b = ++a; // a = 3, b = 3
let x = 0, y = x++, z = ++x;          // y=?, z=?, x=
```

– *Combined numeric and assign operators:* += , -=, *= , /=, %=

```
x += 5;          // equivalent: x = x + 5;
```

– *Unary operators* +, –

Besides keeping (+) or inversing (–) the sign of the variable, the unary operator makes an implicit type conversion whenever mandatory (see the following).

```
let x = 3,
    y = +x,      // -> 3, looks useless,
                 // but informs the engine that typeof y === "number"
    z = -x;      // -> -3
```

WARNING.– Polymorphism of +.

The addition operator + is also a concatenation operator when type is *string*. As soon as a string is found, the rest of the expression is cast to a string, which changes the behavior of next + operators.

```
console.log("3" + 4 + 5);            // "345"
console.log(3 + 4 + "5");            // "75"
console.log(3 + 4 + 5);              // 12
console.log( 248 + "" );         // converts number -> string
console.log(true/2 + "false"); // exercice! do it yourself
```

3.1.3. *Math operations using the methods of the object Math*

The Math object is a built-in object that includes several properties and methods, facilitating the use of mathematical constants and usual mathematical functions.

Properties	Description	Value
Math.E	Number *e*	2.718281828459045
Math.LN10	*Natural logarithm of 10*	2.302585092994046
Math.LN2	Number *natural logarithm of 2*	0.6931471805599453
Math.LOG10E	Number *base 10 logarithm of e*	0.4342944819032518
Math.LOG2E	Number *base 2 logarithm of e*	1.4426950408889634
Math.PI	Number *pi*	3.141592653589793
Math.SQRT1_2	Number	0.7071067811865476
Math.SQRT2	Number	1.4142135623730951

Table 3.2. *Mathematical constants as properties of the Math object*

Methods	Description
`Math.abs()`	Absolute value of *(x)*
`Math.sign()`	Sign of *(x) can be*: 1, −1, 0, −0, NaN
`Math.min()` `Math.max()`	Minimum, maximum of *(x, y)*
`Math.floor()` `Math.ceil()`	Integer, immediately below or above *(x)*

`Math.round()`
`Math.trunc()`
`Math.fround()`
	Rounded integer value or simple truncature of *(x)*
	ou Float simple precision rounded value

`Math.sqrt()` `Math.cbrt()`	Square or cubic root of *(x)*
`Math.hypot()`	Hypotenuse of *(n, m) may generalizes to >2 arguments*
`Math.pow()`	x Power of y *(x, y)*

`Math.cos()`
`Math.sin()`
`Math.tan()`
	Direct trigonometric functions of (x) as "radian": see example below for the conversion [−180,180] -> $[-\pi, \pi]$

`Math.acos()`
`Math.asin()`
`Math.atan()`
`Math.atan?()`
	Inverse trigonometric functions, returns in $[-\pi, \pi]$
	+ atan2(*a, b*) − tangent arc of the ratio *a/b*

`Math.cosh()`
`Math.sinh()`
`Math.tanh()`
	Direct hyperbolic functions
	Ex: Math.cosh(x)= ½($e^x + e^{-x}$)

`Math.acosh()`
`Math.asinh()`
`Math.atanh()`
	Inverse hyperbolic functions
	Ex: x≥1, arcosh(x)=ln(x+ $\sqrt{\{x^2 - 1\}}$)

`Math.exp()` `Math.expm1()`	Exponential of e^x, or e^x - 1 of *(x)*

`Math.log()`
`Math.log1p()`
`Math.log10()`
`Math.log2()`
	Logarithms: natural logarithm of x, natural logarithm of x+1, decimal logarithm, base 2 logarithm of *(x)*

Table 3.3. *Usual mathematical functions as methods of the Math object*

3.1.3.1. *Examples*

– *Converting an angle value from degree to radian*

```
function degToRag(deg) {return deg * Math.PI/180;}
```

– *Getting a random number inside a given positive interval [1, N]*

```
function randomN(n) {return Math.floor( n * Math.random(n) );}
```

3.1.4. *Evaluation in the "numerical context" versus "boolean context"*

When the expression starts with an item of type "number", the rest of the expression is evaluated in "numerical context", and a boolean value will be converted to either 1, if true or 0 if false.

Example:

```
let a = true;                        let b = false;
let y = 1 + a - 12 * b; // -> 2
    y = +a; // -> 1                       y = +b; // -> 0
    y = -a; // -> -1                      y = -b; // -> 0
```

On the other hand, in "boolean context", any value of type "number" is converted to true, including Infinity and -Infinity, with the exception of the values 0, -0 and NaN, which are converted to false:

```
let x = 0;  if(x){ /* code is not executed */ }
    x = 12; if(x){ /* code is executed */ }
```

If, anywhere later in the evaluation of the expression, a type "string" is met, the evaluation switches to "string context", and values true and false become string values:

```
txt = 2 - true +" equals "+ (1 + false);      // 1 equals 1
txt = 2 - true +" equals "+ 1 + false;        // 1 equals 1false
```

3.2. Handling character strings

3.2.1. *Literal notation of strings*

A string literal notation uses quotation marks that can be of three kinds:

– double quotes: `"Candidate";`

– simple quotes: `'500px';`

– or back quotes (aka. backticks):   `` `the value of x is ${x}`. ``

Simple or double quotes play the same role. Combining them is useful when quotes must be used in the string that we write in the literal notation, for instance:

```
"Candidate 'Jean' in Department '2A'"
```

If necessary, the inner quotes can be escaped:

```
"Candidate 'Jean, dit \"Joannot\"' in Department 2A'"
```

– *the associated type is "string"*

```
console.log( typeof "Candidat");      // -> string
console.log( typeof "");              // -> string
```

– *validity of the characters used inside the literal notation*

A string must be composed of valid unicode characters, including whitespaces, special characters, etc., and must be correctly enclosed by appropriate quotes:

```
"the letter π stands for 3.14159"
```

(the Greek letter 'pi' has unicode \u03C0)

3.2.2. Backtick syntax, or template syntax, introduced by ES6

The introduction of this new syntax makes it possible to merge strings and values of expressions, which are evaluated themselves during the evaluation of the whole string. The syntax of the *"template"* part is ${..} and will trigger its evaluation:

```
const cssClassConteneur = "container";
let n = 0; // some index
let htm = `<div class="${cssClassConteneur+n++}"></div>`;
// <div class="container0"></div>, and n = 1
```

3.2.3. *Concatenation operator*

The same sign + is used for number addition and for string concatenation. It is a "polymorphism issue" that is resolved by the script engine, when determining which context is at stake: either a boolean context (only if in a control) or a numerical context or a string context.

3.2.4. *Resolving polymorphism issues with operator + in numerical or string context*

– Let us assume we are not in a control (test in a branch or loop instruction).

– Switching to *string context*:

If the + sign is used as a binary operator between two operands, one of which being a string, then it is interpreted as the "concatenation" operator:

```
let str = "Candidat"; console.log(str + 1);          // -> Candidat1
                      console.log(str + 1+1);        // -> Candidat11
                      console.log(str + (1+1));      // -> Candidat2
                      console.log (str+ 1-1);        // -> NaN
        // beware!: the - sign doesn't work with a string, and
        // the evaluation returns NaN whose type is a number!
```

– Switching to *numerical context*:

If the + sign is used in first position, as a unary operator, it casts the next variable to a valid number or 'NaN' (also a number). Same behavior with the unary − sign:

```
console.log (+1+str);      // -> 1Candidat
console.log (+"1"+2);      // -> 3
console.log (-"1"+2);      // -> 1
console.log (+"a"+2);      // -> NaN
```

EXERCISE.– The inattention leads to the unexpected (explained by the next two lines):

```
(typeof 4 ==="number") + "two".length + typeof 4;// 4number
(typeof 4 ==="number") +""+ "two".length +""+ typeof 4;
                                            // true3number
```

3.2.5. *Behavior of the relational and equality operators*

– Between two numbers, it returns the expected `true` or `false` value.

– Between a `number` and a `string`, a comparison always returns `false`:

```
let str = "abc", n = 2;
console.log(n > str ); // false )  both cases return false
console.log(n < str ); // false )  for uncompatible types
```

– Between two strings, the comparison complies with the unicode order:

The figures [0-9] are lower than all letters:

```
let n = 10, m = 2, str = "abc";
console.log(n > m);                 // true (comparison of numbers)
console.log( n+str > str+n );      // false <- Unicode rule
console.log( n+str < str+n );      // true <- Unicode rule
console.log( n+str > m+str );      // false <- Unicode rule below
// warning: '10abc' > '2abc'       is false
// because the "2" is greater than the "1" of "10"
```

WARNING.– Difference between weak and strict equality operators: `==`, `===` (resp. inequality: `!=`, `!==`)

```
console.log(0x0f == "15");         // true   <= same evaluation
console.log(0x0f === "15");        // false  <= different types
```

This is tedious, for sure, but we must face it in the reality of uses.

3.2.6. *Various facets of string-related issues in a sample application*

The example of enumerating the French "départements" illustrates many issues that are worth mentioning for a data-oriented use of JavaScript. This example is part of one of the applications mentioned in Part 3.

Every department has a name and a code, but the alphabetic order of the names does not exactly follow the numeric order of the codes for various historic reasons:

`"Ain"`: 1, `"Aisne"`: 2, etc ... `"Savoie (Haute)"`: 74, `"Paris"`: 75 (was named `"Seine"` before 1968), etc. ... `"Val-d'Oise"`:95, plus the "ultramar" departments, whose codes start with a Z: `"Guadeloupe"`:`"ZA"`, etc.

Another issue comes from the partitioning, in 1976, of the "Corse" department into "Haute-Corse" and "Corse-du-Sud", with codes "2A" and "2B". The code "20" for "Corse" is not used anymore. All these added oddities hamper a direct sequential encoding of the departments. Let us process the following example:

```
const deps = []; // array for department's data
deps [0]: index 0, name "Ain", code 0 => code = index +1
deps [1]: index 1, name "Aisne", code 2 => code = index +1
...
deps [19]: index 19, name "Haute-Corse", code 2A => code =?f(index)
deps [20]: index 20, name "Corse-du-Sud", code 2B => code =?f(index)
deps [21]: index 21, name "Cote-d'Or", code 21 => code = index
...
```

Therefore, we have four situations:

– from code "1" to "19", index = (+code)-1;

– from "21" to "95", index = (+code);

– special case for the two Corsica departments (codes 2A and 2B)

– special case for the "ultramarin" departments (codes ZA to ZZ)

NOTE.– We use (+code) to force the string code to return a numeric type.

Here is a possible solution for computing the index as a function of the code:

```
const ultramar =
    [95,"ZA","ZB","ZC","ZD","ZM","ZN","ZP","ZS","ZW","ZX","ZZ"];
function getIndexFromCode(code){        // typeof code: 'string'
    let ind;
    const patt1 = /[A-Z]/g;
    if(code.match(patt1)){       // typeof +code not numerical   (1)
        if(code==="2A") ind=19; if(code==="2B") ind=20; //Corse   (2)
        if(code.charAt(0)==="Z"){        // see array ultramar       (3)
            ind = ultramar[0] + ultramar.indexOf(code);
        }
    }else{                               // type of +code is number  (4)
        ind = parseInt(code); // car code est un string
        if(ind<20) ind -= 1;   // de 1-Ain a 19-Correze
```

```
   }
   return ind;
}
```

The logic of the function is:

– check if code contains alpha characters;

– if yes: deal with the "Corse" department (easy) or:

– with "ultramar" departments, using the dedicated array of "code" values:

ultramar[0] = 95; is the number to be added in the instruction: ind = ultramar[0] + ultramar.indexOf(cod); where the method indexOf returns the index of the value in the array.

– otherwise: code can be converted to a number with the method parseInt, which is a method of the global object, such as isNaN(), which we have seen in the previous section.

Let us detail the parseInt and similar parseFloat methods.

parseInt	Result	parseFloat	Result
parseInt("")	NaN	parseFloat("")	NaN
parseInt("042.5km")	42	parseFloat("042.5km")	42.5
parseInt("077")	77 (base 10)	parseFloat("0xF")	0 (no hexa)
parseInt("0xF")	63 (base 8)	parseFloat("2.5e6")	2500000
parseInt("077",8)	15 hexa		

Table 3.4. *Conversion methods parseInt and parseFloat*

NOTE.– The methods parseInt and parseFloat allow us to convert to a numeric value, and the methods isNan and isFinite allow us to check if the variable has one of these special values. Since ES6, these four methods are added to the object Number. For instance, we can use Number.parseInt (code, 10).

3.3. The String.prototype methods

3.3.1. *The need for preprocessing before comparison*

Minor differences, which the human eye directly assimilates, are potential error sources when processing data with a computer. For instance,

"JavaScript" and "Javascript" are not two different languages, and it is mandatory to preprocess strings before comparing them, for instance removing extra spaces or tabs, etc.

Example (using string methods toLowerCase and trim):

```
const str1 = "JavaScript", str2 = " Javascript ";
let s1 = str1.toLowerCase().trim();     // "javascript"
let s2 = str2.toLowerCase().trim();     // "javascript"
console.log( str1 === str2 );   // false
console.log( s1 === s2 );       // true
```

Some natural languages use accentuated characters that, in some circumstances, we may decide to ignore. The string method localeCompare allows us to precisely define what to take into account or not: it can be used with numbers (decimal dot versus comma), dates (several actual formats) and strings with accents:

```
let str1 = "abé", str2 = "àBe";
const compareOpts = {"usage":"search", "sensitivity":"base"}
let n = str1.localeCompare(str2, "fr", compareOpts);
// n = 0 means equal [, 1 greater, -1 lower]
```

The optional arguments in localeCompare(str2 [,locale,opts]) specify the language (here: "fr") and which set of rules to apply for preprocessing:

– "usage":"search" speeds up the comparison if only equality is needed, for no sort is performed, else the default is: "sort" ;

– "sensitivity":"base", means that accents and upper/lower cases are ignored: a=A, a=à, a≠b, else the default is "variant" (i.e. a≠A, a≠à, a≠b).

The method localeCompare solves the lowercase and the accent problems at once. More particular differences can be solved by using the method replace when combined with appropriate regular expressions.

3.3.2. Handling partial comparisons

Partial comparisons may allow us to handle groups of situations. For instance, we can regroup the ultramar departments, or Corsica, by checking only the first character of the string, if it is a "Z", or if it is a "2" followed by a letter:

```
const corse_hte = "2A", corse_sud = "2B", guadeloupe = "ZA";
let str = guadeloupe; console.log(str.charAt(0) === "Z" ); // true
str = corse_sud; console.log(str.charAt(0) === "2" &&
str.charAt(1) >= "A"); // true: [0-9]<[A-Z]<[a-z]
```

3.3.3. *Methods for handling strings*

Methods	Description	Return
str.charAt()	Returns the character at index *(n)*	String
str.charCodeAt()	Returns the UTF-16 code of that character	Number
str.codePointAt()	Returns the unicode point of that character	Number
str.concat()	Combines str with a second *(str2)*	String
str.endsWith() str.startsWith() str.includes()	Checks if the string ends with *(str2)* ... starts with ... or contains	Boolean
str.indexOf() str.lastIndexOf()	Index of the first character = *(str)*, or –1 ... or the last	Number
str.localeCompare()	Comparison according to local rules	(–1,0,1)
str.match()	*see RegExp*	Array
str.normalize()	Normalization unicode	String
str.repeat()	Repeats *(n)* and concats	String
str.replace()	*see RegExp*	String
str.search()	Returns the index of the (pattern) or –1	Number
str.slice() str.substr() str.substring()	Returns a slice between *(start, end)* < *prefer slice* < *prefer slice*	String
str.split()	Splits into an array of strings, wrt *(separator)*	Array
str.toLocaleLowerCase() str.toLocaleUpperCase() str.toLowerCase() str.toUpperCase()	Returns a modified string	String
str.trim()	Returns a string without spaces around	String

Table 3.5. *Methods of the prototype of the object string*

The built-in String object has been designed to support a bunch of methods, which will be delegated to any string, with the help of an associated object String.prototype. This *delegation* mechanism will be detailed later. Table 3.5 provides a list of the methods of the String.prototype object.

Let us detail some of the methods listed.

3.3.3.1. *Slice(start, end)*

The indices (start,end) are consistently handled, returning the empty string if start ≥ end, and allowing negative values to count backward from the end.

```
let str = 'The morning is upon us.'; // str.length : 23.
str.slice(1, 8);        // -> 'he morn'
str.slice(8, -2);       // -> 'ing is u'
str.slice(12);          // -> 'is upon us.' (up to the end)
str.slice(30);          // -> '' (... au-delà de 23)
str.slice(-3);          // -> 'us.' (up to the end)
str.slice(0, -2);       // -> 'The morning is upon u'
```

NOTE.– The methods slice, substr, substring are similar (competing for historical reasons). The method slice has the most consistent use of start, end and negative values: just avoid the other two.

3.3.3.2. *Concat(second)*

```
console.log("Good".concat(" Morning")); // Good Morning
```

3.3.3.3. *Split(separator)*

This is very useful for transforming a string into an array of strings controlled by the separator argument.

EXAMPLE.– Using split to process CSV data ("Comma Separated Values").

```
const schemaCSV = "Id#, Product, Unit Price";
const schemaTable = schemaCSV.split(", ");
      // ["Id#", "Product", "Unit Price"]
```

The separator can be a string, such as that previously mentioned, or a regular expression (see the following) in which case, the use of parentheses has a meaning: "capturing parentheses". The separator itself is added to the returned array.

EXAMPLE.– The regular expression searches the "digits" (code = \d) and splits:

```
const str = 'Hello 1 word. Sentence 2.';
let split = str.split(/\d/);    // no parenthesis ->
      // split: ["Hello ", " word. Sentence ", "."]
split = str.split(/(\d)/);      // with parentheses ->
      // split: ["Hello ", "1", " word. Sentence ", "2", "."]
```

3.3.4. *Regular expressions*

Regular expressions are "patterns" that describe how a string is made of parts, and we can use them to retrieve any subchain made the same way.

Their esoteric aspect makes them repulsive, which leads to neglect them. But they are very useful in combination with the "string methods": match, replace, search and split.

Regular expressions can be written as:

– in literal notation: `const patt = /http/gm;`.

– With constructor: `const patt = new RegExp("http",flg);`.

`flg`, optional, can be: `let flg = "gm";` (which means: global + multiline)

Any object patt inherits from the object RegExp.prototype.

Methods	Description	Retour
`patt.test()`	Checks the pattern in the string *(str)*	Boolean
`patt.exec()`	Returns an array depending on *(str)*	Array

Table 3.6. Methods of RegExp.prototype

3.3.5. *Evaluation and uses*

– It is used directly as an object receiving a method, for example:

```
const patt = /http/;           // pattern 'http', no modifier
patt.test("http://www.w3shools.com");   // -> true
```

– Also as an argument of a string method, for example:

```
const patt = /\d/g; // pattern '\d', modifier : g = 'global'
const str = "la date du 14 juillet<br>";
let tab, msg = str;
while ((tab = patt.exec(str)) !== null) {
    msg += 'match ' + tab[0] + ', at index: ' + tab.index +"<br>";
}
console.log( msg + str.replace(patt, "#"));
/* displays:
        la date du 14 juillet
        match 1, at index: 11
        match 4, at index: 12
        la date du ## juillet
```

3.3.6. *Some examples of useful patterns*

```
const pattHexa = [0-9a-fA-F]+           // hexadecimal integer
const pattIPad = (\d{1,3}\.){3}\d{1,3}   // simple IP address
```

Breaking down the hexadecimal pattern:

– 0–9: seeks for a digit;

– a–f: seeks for a letter between a and f, idem with A–F;

– the square brackets: seek for characters of one of the previous kind;

– the trailing + sign means any number of occurrences, at least one;

– for example: `pattHexa.test("2Abd");   // -> true`.

Breaking down the IP address pattern:

– seeking for a group of 1–3 digits: use (\d) for one digit and a repeat factor {1,3} between a minimum and a maximum. This gives: (\d){1,3}, or simply \d{1,3} because \d is a primitive sign, it does not require the parentheses;

– seeking for three times such a group, followed by a dot, plus once more, without the dot: let us add the dot: (\d{1,3}\.) and the parentheses are required here, then again a repeat factor {3}, just three times, plus a fourth and last group: (\d{1,3}\.){3}\d{1,3}

NOTE.– The dot is the sign for "any" character, therefore we must "escape" it: \. to ensure that we are really seeking for a dot and not for any character.

3.3.7. *General syntax of a regular expression*

3.3.7.1. *The "pattern"*

This is delimited by slash signs / ... / and can be followed by a modifier, which is one or several letters among which: "g" for global (every occurrence of the pattern in the string), "i" for insensitive to upper-/lowercase and "m" for multiline.

3.3.7.2. *The characters*

The characters that we expect to individually match can be any character, except the seven listed below, which must be "escaped" (backslashed), plus, depending on the context, the parentheses and square brackets:

?	.	$	+	*	/	\	(..)	[..]
\?	\.	\$	\+	*	\/	\\	(\..\)	\[..\]

3.3.7.3. *The classes of alternative signs*

Instead of checking the signs individually, we can check a sign among a class of alternative signs delimited by brackets [..]. For example:

```
[abc]      means either a, b or c
[a-zA-Z]   means any character between a and z or between A and Z
```

– we can use shortcuts for some usual classes:

```
\d   instead of   [0-9],
\w   instead of   [a-zA-Z0-9_]
\s   instead of   [ \t\r\n\v\f]   spaces, tabs, line-feeds ...
```

– we can negate a group with [^..];

– we negate a shortcut with the corresponding uppercase letter: \D to negate \d;

– we can form a subpattern by using parentheses (..) and we can number them from 1 to 9, for a further use, or avoid numbering them with a ? mark: (?:..);

– we can accept a repeated subpattern, exactly *n* times, at least minimum times, or between minimum and maximum times: (..){n} (..){min,}   (..){min,max};

– [*several more features can be found documented on the Internet ...*].

3.3.8. *Combining RegExp and String.prototype methods*

3.3.8.1. *String.prototype.replace()*

For example, multitarget reformating. For instance, we want to prepare a string that can be formatted later for HTML display or simple text display. This can be done easily by using some predefined custom mark (here: §§§) to tell when reformatting must occur. Then, different formats may be applied:

```
const str = "sub-paragraph 1§§§sub-paragraph 2§§§sub-paragraph 3";
let htm = "<p>" + str.replace(/§§§/g, "<br>"); + "</p>";
let txt = str.replace(/§§§/g, "\n"); + "\n";
```

3.3.8.2. *String.prototype.match(), String.prototype.search()*

These two methods are straightforward (see also metaprogramming with symbols in Chapter 7.

Objects and Prototypes

JavaScript distinguishes itself from most usual "object-oriented programming" (OOP) languages, which are "class based": JavaScript is "prototype based". This originality is confusing for people accustomed to other OOP languages, and sometimes perceived as a weakness vis-à-vis better "controlled" languages such as Java, of which it "inherited" the name based on a misunderstanding.

4.1. Introduction

This chapter is organized as follows:

– an introduction about the notions of "*concept*" versus "*named entities*" should help in understanding the difference between "class-based" and "prototype-based" OOP;

– section 4.2: This section details the syntax and use of the "object literal" in JavaScript, popular through the JSON format, which is widely used to exchange data over the Internet;

– section 4.3: This section deals with the methods of the built-in objects "Object" and "Object.prototype", how they provide the notion of inheritance by delegation and how objects can be related;

– section 4.4: After analyzing the role of prototypes, we detail the three approaches for creating objects:

- literal: this includes the operator {..}, the role of the functions Object and Function, to enlighten the role of the "prototypes" in the inheritance mechanism in JavaScript,

- prototypal: this includes the innovative methods Object.create and Object.assign (ES6),

- classical: this consists of the operator "new" and the "constructor" functions.

We can hardly talk about objects without talking about functions, and even arrays. Therefore, Chapters 5–7 are very intertwined. But "object" is probably the most basic notion, and we start with it, even if several "forward references" must be used in the text to point out that some tools will be defined later on.

The prototypal approach may seem puzzling, but it provides flexibility and ease in programming (maybe too much?). We do hope that this chapter will convince you that it is better to stand with the very nature of JavaScript, and use the prototypal approach instead of the classical one, as often as possible, and especially for the kind of "data-oriented" applications targeted by this book.

4.2. The objects: concepts versus named entities

An object is something that we can grasp (a glass on a table), distinguish at a glance (a cloud in the sky) or which we can describe by some characteristics (an appointment with a friend). In any language, an object is either a particular object (this glass on this table), or the generic concept that we attach to a set of similar particular objects ("a" glass).

These two viewpoints may be as old as any human language: is the generic concept different from the set of the named entities it represents? (see Plato's "Cave allegory", the "problem of universals"). The computer languages face the same issue:

– should we create a generic representation (a "class") from which to create particular "instances"?

– should we use a particular object to represent all objects similar to it?

A metaphor may help identify the issue: let us dare to quote the field of law: exclusive use of Jurisprudence (any case may be used *a posteriori*) versus exclusive use of the Civil Code (any case reduces to an article of the Code).

We propose to rephrase the distinction between:

Generic concept, an *a priori* representation of similar objects, made of:

– an (abstract) structure, probably a tree-structure, of named containers;

– an operator to create instances;

– the ability to modify, augment, the objects after their creation.

Named entities, represented by an explicit notation:

– an (explicit) structure of named containers with a defined content;

– a link to the reference of the set of similar objects.

Let us first study how JavaScript answers the named entity notion.

4.3. Object literal notation in JavaScript

A JavaScript object is merely the container of a collection of named values. Here is the syntax of the notation representing such a collection.

4.3.1. *Syntax for "object literal":*

The operator typeof answers "object" to every notation complying with the following syntax (object notation):

– the container is delimited by curly braces { ... }:

```
{} is the empty object
```

– the inside collection is made of comma separated "properties";

– a property is a couple "property_name": "value":

```
{ "key_1" : "value_1", "key_2" : "value_2", ... }
```

– a key can be used with or without "quotes";

– a value must comply with the requirements of any variable value: primitive value, literal: number, string, another object, including array and function, or more complex expression. Object literals can be nested (see the following).

This notation is simple, but may present some traps: here are several warnings to help you to avoid writings that will mislead the interpreter.

4.3.2. *Important warnings about writing JavaScript object notation*

4.3.2.1. *The name of the properties*

Any Unicode character can be used, and any word, including "reserved word". However, we recommend to respect these best practices:

– start with a letter (or possibly a dollar sign $ or underscore _);

– preferably do not use reserved words;

– preferably use quotes, for they are mandatory in the JSON format.

Examples of valid property names, complying best practice:

```
{ "firstName": "Jean", "name2": "O", "_salaire_€": 20e3, ...
```

4.3.2.2. *The type and value of properties*

The type of the property is the type of its value (idem: variables):

– string: (idem variables) the engine store, the string and the address (reference) becomes the value of the property.

```
"first": "Jean",      // address of the string "Jean"
```

– number or boolean: the primitive values must be written without quotes, unless they are strings and a conversion may be necessary:

```
"age": 22,      // type number
"age": "22",    // type string: to convert if required
```

– object (including array): any value whose typeof is "object" is valid:

```
"circonscription": { "dept": "Gironde", "numero": 2 }
"affiliation": [ "party_1", "party_2" ]
```

These literals are stored and their references become the values.

– function: any function expression, then called a "*method*":

```
fullName: function(){return this.first +" "+ this.last;}
```

The methods are not accepted in JSON format, only as strings:

```
fullName: "function(){return this.first +' '+ this.last;}"
```

4.3.3. *The object literal first use: to define an object type variable*

An object literal on the right-hand side of a variable definition statement is stored, and the address is assigned to the (left-hand) variable. Example:

```
const candidatN = {
        "first": "Jean", "last": "Dupont",
        "age": 22,
        "circonscription": {
                "dept": "Gironde", "numero": 2
        },
        "fullName": function(){return this.first+" "+this.last;}
};
```

The object is created when the engine meets the curly braces {.}: the built-in function Object is implicitly invoked. The keyword this will be explained later.

4.3.4. *The object literal second use: data notation in JSON format*

The object literal is a mere character string that we can archive in a plain text file. The further reading of the file will provide a string that could be directly used as the literal for an object in the target code, written in JavaScript or possibly some other programming language: the chapter on AJAX details this importation mechanism.

This idea of a plain text file for the object notation has been specified by Douglas Crockford in 2001, precisely "Java Script Object Notation" (JSON). Since then, it has been massively used as an exchange format over the Internet. To facilitate the interface with those "JSON files", an object JSON has been added to JavaScript, with two static methods:

– JSON.parse() interprets the string as a literal and returns the object.

– JSON.stringify() converts an object into a string, keeping only the "enumerable properties", and making some editing (see below).

```
const candidatN = {
        "first": "Jean", "last": "Dupont", "age": undefined,
        "circ": {
                dept: "Gironde", num: 2
        },
        "fullN" : function(){return this.first +" "+ this.last;}
};
JSON.stringify(candidatN);
//prints:
{"first":"Jean","last":"Dupont","circ":{"dept":"Gironde","num":2}}
```

NOTE.– White spaces or line feeds are removed, quotes are added (dept, num), and the method is ignored, as well as the property whose value is undefined.

4.3.5. *Accessing the individual properties of an object*

There are two notations to denote one particular property of an object:

– dot notation: candidatN.first; NB: property name without quotes;

– bracket notation: candidat ["first"]; NB: property name with quotes.

```
let dN = candidatN.circo.dept;
    dN = candidatN["circo"]["dept"];
```

The dot notation is simpler, but cannot be used in every case, in particular if the name of the property is given through a variable. For example:

```
function f(prop){
    candidatN[prop];   // ok, if prop exists in candidatN
    candidatN.prop;    // undefined : "prop" isn't a property
}
f("first");    // gives prop, in f, the value "first"
```

4.3.5.1. *Using references in the object literal*

For instance, with the nested object "circo", we can create the object once, outside of any "candidat" object, then the reference to that "circo" object can be mutualized between several "candidat-like" objects. To mutualize avoids creating multiple instances of the "Gironde" string, and makes it possible to "inherit" further additions, modifications brought to the mutualized reference:

```
const circo_3302 = {    // (Gironde INSEE number is 33)
            "dept": "Gironde", "num": 2
      };
const candidatN = {
      "first": "Jean", "last": "Dupont", "circo": circo_3302
};
circo_3302.population = 25600;
candidatN.circo.population   // 25600 new property is "concatenated"
```

4.3.6. *Notation syntax evolution with ES6*

Regular notation	ES6 shorthand

`let a = [[value]];`
`const obj = {`
  `a: a,`
  `foo: function() {...}`
`};`
	`let a = [[value]];`
	`const obj = {`
	  `a,`
	  `foo() {...}`
	`};`

	A declared and defined variable can be used directly as a property. Methods are named directly.

Table 4.1. *Shorthand syntax for object literal notation (ES6)*

Using JSON.stringify(obj) restores the regular JSON notation. For example:

```
let a = "A", b = 1;
JSON.stringify({a, b});         // {"a":"A","b":1}
JSON.stringify({a:a, b:b});     // {"a":"A","b":1} : identical
```

4.4. The built-in methods of Object and Object.prototype

4.4.1. *The methods of Object, Object.prototype, and JSON*

Table 4.2 lists the "static methods" of the built-in object Object, which must be invoked directly from Object: Object.*method*().

Method	Description	Return
Object.assign	Copies the enumerable own properties of (o1,o2 ...	Object
Object.create	Creates an object whose prototype is (proto)	Object
Object.defineProperties Object.defineProperty	Creates or modifies the properties of (o) Idem. only one property	Object
Object.freeze Object.isFrozen	Prevent against modifications of (o) Test status	Object Boolean
Object.getPrototypeOf Object.setPrototypeOf	Returns the *[[prototype]]* of (o) [to avoid : instead use Object.create()]	Object
Object.keys Object.values Object.entries	lists names of enumerable own properties of (o), idem for values, idem for [key, value]	Array

Table 4.2. *The most usual static methods of Object*

Table 4.3 lists the methods of the object Object.prototype, which are delegated to all objects. They are invoked from any object: obj.method().

Method	Description	Return
obj.hasOwnProperty	Tests if property (*p*) is "own"	Boolean
obj.isPrototypeOf	Tests if prototype chain contains (*o1*)	Boolean
obj.propertyIsEnumerable	Tests if property (*p*) is "enumerable"	Boolean
obj.toString obj.toLocaleString	Provides a stringified version of the object (idem with locale rules)	String

Table 4.3. *The methods of Object.prototype, delegated to any object*

And, it is worth remembering here the two (static) methods of the object JSON.

Method	Description	Return
JSON.parse()	Transforms a valid JSON notation into an object	Object
JSON.stringify()	Gives the string JSON notation from an object	String

Table 4.4. *Static methods of JSON*

4.4.2. *Create an object and specify its properties*

Here is the syntax of the two most useful methods:

Object.assign(target, source [, source2, ...])   makes it possible to "augment" the object "target" with the properties of another object "source" (or several). Returns the augmented "target".

Object.create(proto [, descriptor1, descriptor2, ...]) creates an object from the object "proto" used as the prototype of the new object. The (optional) descriptors make it possible to add individual properties with specific control attributes.

The two methods `Object.defineProperty( obj, prop, descriptor )`, and `Object.defineProperties( obj, objectWithDescibedProps )` also utilize the "descriptors" properties, as described below.

4.4.3. *Syntax and usage of the "descriptor" property*

In the methods described in the following, Descriptors have been added to JavaScript by ES5, to better control the rights (e.g. read/write) of every property. All the descriptors possess:

– `configurable`: the descriptor itself can be modified and the property can be deleted "delete" (default: false);

– `enumerable`: the property is enumerable (default: `false`).

Then two cases (exclusives): the "data descriptors" with:

– `value`: the value of the property (default: `undefined`);

– `writable`: the property can be modified (default: `false`);

and the "accessor descriptors" instead have:

– `get`: function returning the value of the property (def.: `undefined`);

– `set`: function whose argument becomes the value (def.: `undefined`).

Using a "data descriptor":

```
{ "property name" : {               "value": value,
                                    "enumerable": boolean,
                                    "configurable": boolean,
                                    "writable": boolean }
}
```

By default, all three booleans are initialized to `false`.

WARNING.– For an object created by a literal, only the couple (key, value) is considered, and by default, all three booleans are initialized to `true`.

The Object.freeze(obj) method prevents any modification of the object, which constant does not do.

The methods `Object.getPrototypeOf(obj)`, `obj.isPrototypeOf(obj2)`, `obj.hasOwnProperty(p)`, `obj.propertyIsEnumerable(p)`, and `Object.getOwnPropertyNames(obj)` are obvious.

`Object.getOwnPropertyNames` and similar methods can be added which make it possible to list otherwise invisible properties (not of use in this work).

4.4.4. *Listing the properties of an object, analyzing a literal*

4.4.4.1. *Using the instruction for...in*

There exists a property enumeration instruction in JavaScript: `for..in`

```
const candidatN = {"first": "Jean", "last": "Dupont", ... ...};
for (let prop in candidatN) {console.log(prop);}
for (let prop in candidatN) {console.log(candidatN[prop]);}
// these instruction lines successively display:
        "first", "last", "age", "circonscrition"
        "Jean", "Dupont", 22, [Object()]
```

NOTE 1.– `for..in` looks like a loop, but it is an *enumerator*: it lists the enumerable properties of the object, either own properties or delegated by the prototype. To break down between own/delegated properties, use `obj.hasOwnProperty(prop)`.

NOTE 2.– for..in is not recursive, for a nested object, you must code recursively.

4.4.4.2. Using the static methods of Object

Object.keys(obj)/.values/.entries returns an array of the enumerable properties of obj in the same order than for..in but limited to each property: keys returns the names, values the values and entries the couples. Let us compare:

```
for (let p in candidatN) {
        if(candidatN.hasOwnProperty(p)){console.log(candidatN[p]);}
}
// equivalent to:
Object.values(candidatN).forEach(function(v){console.log( v );};
```

4.4.4.3. Methods of JSON object (with option function)

The JSON methods accept a second, optional, argument: a function with two arguments (key, value).

For example, with 'JSON.stringify' we cannot directly "stringify" a method, but we can get its code as plain text::

```
function stringifyTheMethods(k, v) {
        return (typeof v === "function")? v.toString(): v;
});
JSON.stringify(candidatN, stringifyTheMethods);
// yields:
{"first":"Jean","last":"Dupont","circo":{"dept":"Gironde","num":2},"fullName
":"function() {return this.first +\" \"+ this.last;}"}
```

NOTE.– The quotes used in the code are escaped.

For example, with 'JSON.parse', to avoid warning messages ("JSON badly formed"), we can add escapements for tabulations, line breaks, etc., with regular expressions::

```
function escapeSpecialChars(k, v) {
        return v.replace(/\"/g, "\\"")    // quotes
                .replace(/\n/g, "\\n")    // line feed
                .replace(/\r/g, "\\r")    // carriage return
                .replace(/\b/g, "\\b")    // back space
```

```
                .replace(/\t/g, "\\t")   // horizontal tab
                .replace(/\f/g, "\\f"); // new page
}
JSON.parse( jsonText, escapeSpecialChars );
```

4.5. Basics of the "prototypal approach" in JavaScript

JavaScript takes into account the notion of "named entity":

– the object literal provides the means to create individual objects;

– the JSON notation makes it possible to archive and to reuse such objects, including with different languages, for instance Python, or usual speadsheets.

Question:

Does JavaScript take into account the notion of "generic concept"?

And by which means?

Many OOP languages use a software feature, named a "*class*", to represent the *generic concept*, plus a mechanism to build "*instances*" of that class, which are the *named entities*. In JavaScript, there is no such thing as a class, neither an instance: So, what do we do?

NOTE.– The ambition of Netscape was to have a scripting language similar to Java. Brendan Eich, in order to complete his contract during the very short allotted time, chose the "prototypal approach", which is to say: the mere addition, in every object, of a link to another object, named its "prototype". This simple choice has since fueled many misunderstandings, especially because of the operator: "new". Despite the introduction of the keyword "class" in ES6, nothing has changed: classes and instances still do not exist in JavaScript.

Does the "prototypal approach" answer the three earlier mentioned criteria for generic concepts ? Does it provide:

– a tree structure of named containers?

– a means to build named entities of a given model?

– the ability to modify, or to augment the objects, once having been created?

4.5.1. *JavaScript object's fundamental relation: "has prototype"*

Instead of being member of a *"class"*, every JavaScript object owns a link to a particular object: its *"prototype"*. Though it is a property of the object, this link is not directly accessible (not part of the norm). Let us name this link: *[[prototype]]*.

Figure 4.1 demonstrates the fundamental power and limits of this relation.

Every object owns *one and only one* *[[prototype]]*. That uniqueness induces a functional relation, namely $\rightarrow_{[[prototype]]}$

> $\forall x,\ object,\ \exists p,\ object,\ such\ that\ x \rightarrow_{[[prototype]]} p.$
>
> which reads: "x has prototype p". It can be written: *[[prototype]](x)=p*, because it is a functional relation

From that functional relation we can derive an equivalence relation: $\approx$

> $x \approx y \Leftrightarrow \exists p,\ [[prototype]](x)=p\ \&\ [[prototype]](y)=p$
> (x equivalent to y, if and only if x and y have the same prototype)

Every equivalence class can be named with the name of the prototype:

> $x \approx_p y \Leftrightarrow [[prototype]](x) = [[prototype]](y) = p$

One particular equivalence class is the class of all objects built from an object literal: in which case p = Object.prototype,

> $x \approx_{Object.prototype} y \Leftrightarrow [[prototype]](x) = [[prototype]](y) =$ Object.prototype

That Object.prototype, is the only object to have null as prototype:

> *[[prototype]]*(Object.prototype*)*= null
> (Remember: typeof null === "object")

From the functional relation *[[proto]]* we can derive a strict partial order: $\neg$

> $x \neg y \Leftrightarrow y = [[prototype]](x),\ or = [[prototype]](...([[prototype]](x)...)$

That order yields a tree structure, where every object is part of a particular branch of that tree, named its "prototype chain".

Figure 4.1. *The maths behind the prototype: two dual relations and a tree structure*

So far, we know how to build objects from literals. Now, the question is:

How can we build an object with a given object as its prototype?

Since ES6, there is a simple answer: thanks to the method `Object.create`, we can pick an object and use it as the prototype for the new object:

```
const proto = {/* any object, e.g. a literal */};
const newob = Object.create(proto);    // newob.[[prototype]] = proto
```

The strict partial order ¬ and the associated tree structure determine the *"prototype chain"* of every object. To keep it simple, let us say that any JavaScript object is built:

– either from a literal, and its *[[prototype]]* is `Object.prototype`:

{ ...... } ¬ Object.prototype ¬ null

– or from `Object.create(proto)`, and its *[[prototype]]* is proto:

x ¬ proto ¬ ... ¬ Object.prototype ▢ null

The overall tree structure is made up of nodes that are prototypes, except the terminal leaves, and its root is `Object.prototype` (we can ignore `null`). All nodes, which are neither root, nor leaves, can be labeled by the prototype that is characteristic of the related *"equivalence class"*.

We can say that these equivalence classes are the *"generic concepts"* we were looking for in the previous section, and, at the same time, any such *generic concept* is also a *"named entity"*, for the prototype is an object (remember the similarity with "jurisprudence").

4.5.2. *Role of the prototypes and inheritance mechanism*

Given an object (p), it is by itself a *named entity*, and can play the role of a *generic concept* for other objects (x):   x ¬ p

The method `Object.create(p)` allows us to create one x whose prototype is p, and `Object.getPrototypeOf(x)` allows us to check if the prototype is p:

```
const p = { oprint(){return 'I am p the prototype';} };
const x = Object.create(p);
if(Object.getPrototypeOf(x) === p){console.log(x.oprint());}
        // " I am p the prototype " (the test is positive)
```

Let us create a new object using x as prototype:

```
const y = Object.create(x);
if(Object.getPrototypeOf(y) === x){console.log(y.oprint());}
        // " I am p the prototype " (the test is also positive)
```

The objects x and y successively inherit the method oprint from p. The relation is transitive and the chain of prototypes is:

```
y x ¬ p ¬ Object.prototype
```

And inheritance is transitive as well: the object that plays the role of prototype automatically delegates its methods and properties to the members of the equivalence class, which it labels.

This "inheritance by delegation" works as follows:

When a property is "called" on an object x, for instance through the dot notation x.oprint, then the property is searched among x's own properties. If not found, the same search is performed for each member of the prototype chain down to Object.prototype. The first occurrence found becomes the value, else undefined is the value.

4.5.2.1. Conclusion

With the object notation {..} we can create objects whose prototype is Object.prototype.

With the Object.create(p) method, we can create objects whose prototype is the object p, which therefore becomes a prototype unbeknownst to itself.

The prototypes chain is also an inheritance chain: the properties of an object playing the role of a prototype are delegated to all the objects upwards in the chain.

The inheritance by delegation is dynamic: any modification of a method of a certain prototype object automatically modifies the method used by any object that has the prototype in its chain.

NOTE.– By contrast, a method is "static" if that method is owned by the object itself.

JavaScript is very permissive; it is sometimes unwise to use this flexibility: some recommendations are as follows:

RECOMMENDATION 1.– Objects are containers, the contents can be modified, but do not modify the box: use const x = Object.create(p); or const x = {..}; to declare and create an object.

RECOMMENDATION 2.– Its prototypes chain is the marker of an object; do not modify that chain once created and do not use Object.setPrototypeOf(x).

In the following, three object construction approaches are described: *literal* with the operator {..}, *prototypal* with Object.create and *classical* with the operator new.

4.5.3. *Object construction: the "literal approach"*

To better understand object construction, we need some additional background.

4.5.3.1. *The object–function "Function"*

The built-in object Function is a function, and as such (see chapter 5) it owns a special property named prototype, which is not to be confused with the *[[prototype]]* property. Hence Function owns a Function.prototype and a *[[prototype]]*.

4.5.3.2. *The object–function "Object"*

The built-in object Object is a function, therefore it owns an Object.prototype, which points to the root to any prototypes chain, and whose *[[prototype]]* is null.

4.5.3.3. *The operator {..}*

The literal approach for creating an object is: const x = {..}; it:

– creates a new object x: implicitly with function Object;

– sets the prototype: x.*[[prototype]]* = Object.prototype;

– sets constructor's name: x.constructor.name = "Object".

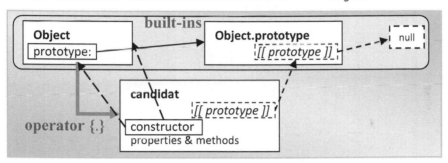

Figure 4.2. *The diagram of the literal object*

Once created, the object may receive new properties, and others can be modified·

```
const x = {last: "Dupont", first:"J"};
x.first = "Jean";
x.full = function(){return this.first+" "+this.last}
```

NOTE.– These properties and methods are named "*static*" and we must use the object itself to modify them. By contrast, properties or methods delegated from the prototype can be modified independently.

4.5.4. *Object construction: the "prototypal approach"*

Any object, created with the literal approach, can be used to create a new object whose *[[prototype]]* is that first object:

```
const protox =    {last = "Dupont", first = "Jean";
                   full(){return this.first+" "+this.last}};
const x = Object.create(protox);
console.log(x.full());              // Jean Dupont
if(Object.getPrototypeOf(x) === protox)   // true
     console.log(x.constructor.name);     // Object
```

The method 'Object.create' acts as follows:

– creates a new object x;

– set: x.*[[prototype]]* = protox;

– the property x.constructor inherits from protox.constructor.

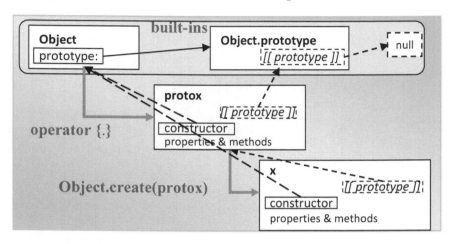

Figure 4.3. *The diagram of the object created from a prototype*

4.5.5. *The pattern "assign/create"*

```
function Candidat(){}   // provides Candidat.prototype
Candidat.prototype.full = function(){return this.first+ ... };
const x = Object.assign(                        // line 3
                   Object.create(Candidat.prototype),
                   {last = "Dupont", first = "Jean"} );
console.log(x.full());                      //-> Jean Dupont
if(Object.getPrototypeOf(x) === Candidat.prototype) //true
     console.log(x.constructor.name);     //-> Candidat
```

The combination Object.assign/Object.create (lines 3–5) underlines the distinction between the "*generic concept*" (the argument of 'create') and the "*named entity*" (arguments 2+ of 'assign'). We call it the *assign/create pattern* (see "Design patterns" in Chapter 7 for more details).

The method Object.assign adds new properties, or modifies existing ones according to its arguments 2 and next. To remove an existing property, we need to apply the operator 'delete' on that property. The property constructor has been valuated to Candidat by Object.create.

Further adding of methods to Candidat.prototype will automatically trigger those methods for every object created through the assign/create combo.

In Part 3, this pattern is put into practice with several "data-oriented" applications.

4.5.6. *Object construction: the "classical approach"*

4.5.6.1. *What does the JavaScript operator new do?*

It invokes a function, which is named a "constructor". Good practice is to capitalize its name with an uppercase letter:

```
function Candidat(last){this.last = last;}          // line 1
const x = new Candidat("Dupont");                   // line 2
```

Line 1. Two objects are created: Candidat and Candidat.prototype.

WARNING.– The property Candidat.*[[prototype]]* is Function.prototype, for Candidat is a function, which inherits function's methods: e.g. call.

Line 2, new Candidat, acts as follows:

– creates a new object x, which is assigned to the pronoun this, inside the function. Otherwise, this = window (or the global object);

– returns implicitly this (unless an explicit return is coded: to avoid!);

– updates x.*[[prototype]]* = Candidat.prototype, which makes x inherit by delegation;

– updates x.constructor = Candidat.

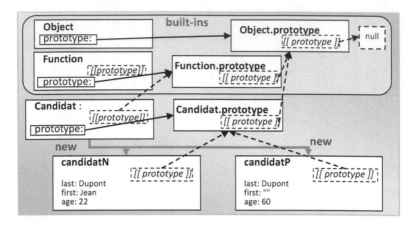

Figure 4.4. *The diagram of the object created by a constructor*

The role of the constructor is very limited: the object Candidat.prototype is the one that really triggers the inheritance by delegation. The overall *classical* operation[1] is complex, even if it is transparent for the programmer.

4.6. Comparing "prototypal" and "classical" approaches

Let's explore the arguments of Douglas Crockford[2], who advocated the introduction of Object.create

> In a prototypal system, objects inherit from objects. JavaScript, however, lacks an operator that performs this operation. Instead it has a *new* operator, such that:
>
> new f() produces a new object that inherits from f.prototype
>
> This indirection was intended to make the language seem more familiar to classically trained programmers, but failed to do that, as we can see from the very low opinion Java programmers have of JavaScript. JavaScript's constructor pattern did not appeal to the classical crowd. It also obscured JavaScript's true prototypal nature. As a result, there are very few programmers who know how to use the language effectively.
>
> Fortunately, it is easy to create an operator that implements true prototypal inheritance
> newObject = Object.create(oldObject);

---

1 Adjective "classical" here: means "usual" and "class mimicking".
2 2008-04-07, http://javascript.crockford.com/prototypal.html.

He was simulating that method[3] using the operator new:

```
Object.create = function (proto) {
    function F() {}              // creates a prototype property
    F.prototype = proto;         // makes proto that prototype
    return new F();      // creates an object with proto as prototype
};
```

4.6.1. *Simulating a class hierarchy in JavaScript*

A class hierarchy is based upon the "*Is-a*" relation, for example, "a candidate is-a person" (plus some specific properties). Let us compare the two approaches.

4.6.1.1. *Classical simulation: class "Person" and subclass "Candidate"*

```
function Person (last, first) {                          // line 1
    this.last = last || "?";
    this.first = first || "";
}
function Candidate (last, first, dN) {                   // line 2
    Person.call(this, last, first); // uses code of Person with this
    this.dN = dN || "somewhere";
}
Candidate.prototype = new Person();                     // line 3
Candidate.prototype.constructor = Candidate;            // line 4
Person.prototype.fullName = function(){                 // line 5
    return this.first+" "+this.last;
};
Candidate.prototype.fullName = function(){              // line 6
    return Person.prototype.fullName.call(this)+", at "+this.dN;
};
const c1 = new Person("D","Jean", "Creuse");
const c2 = new Candidate("D","Jean", "Creuse");
```

Let us comment on the logics of that code:

– lines 1 and 2, the functions Person and Candidate are creating prototypes, and make some initializations;

– line 2: Candidate "recycles" the code of Person with itself (this), i.e. the object that will be created when invoking new Candidate(). This is the job of Person.call (see Chapter 6).

---

3 Since then, Object.create was added to ES5 and Object.assign to ES6.

– line 3: links Candidate to the prototypes chain of Person:

    `c2 ⌐ Candidate.prototype ⌐ Person.prototype ⌐ Object.prototype`

– line 4: updates property `constructor`, which line 3 initialized to Person;

– line 5: adds method `fullName` to `Person.prototype`;

– line 6: recycles the code `Person.fullName` in `Candidate.prototype`.

The inheritance is controlled in lines 3-4. Finally, for c1, c2, let's print: '`c.constructor.name`', `JSON.stringify(c)` and `c.fullName()`:

name	JSON	fullName()
Person	{"last":"D","first":"Jean"}	Jean D
Candidate	{"last":"D","first":"Jean","dN":"Creuse"}	Jean D, en Creuse

4.6.1.2. *Prototypal simulation: class "Person" and subclass "Candidate"*

```
function Person(){}                                    // line 1
function Candidate(){}                                 // line 2
Person.prototype.fullName = function(){                // line 3
    return this.first+" "+this.last;
};
Candidate.prototype = Object.assign(                   // line 4
            Object.create(Person.prototype),
            { fullName(){
    return Person.prototype.fullName.call(this)+", at "+this.dN;
}});
Candidate.prototype.constructor = Candidate;           // line 5
const p1 = Object.assign(                              // line 6
            Object.create(Person.prototype),
            { last:"D", first:"Jean", dN:"Creuse"});
const p2 = Object.assign(                              // line 7
            Object.create(Candidate.prototype),
            { last:"D", first:"Jean", dN:"Creuse"});
```

Let us comment and compare:

– lines 1 and 2, functions `Person` and `Candidat` merely create prototypes;

– line 3: adds `fullName` to `Person.prototype` (= line 5 classical);

– line 4: the assign/create pattern modifies `Candidate.prototype` to inherit from `Person.prototype`, and updates method `fullName` (= line 6 classical);

– line 5: updates `Candidate.prototype.constructor` (= line 4 classical).

Figures 4.5 and 4.6 demonstrate the similarity of the two approaches.

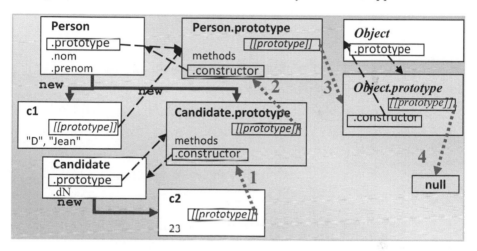

Figure 4.5. *Subclassing in the classical approach*

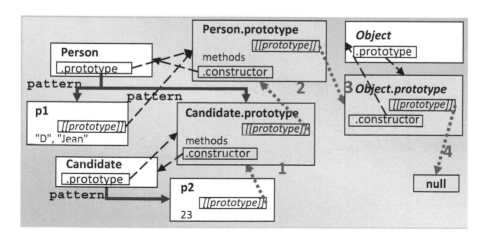

Figure 4.6. *Subclassing in the prototypal approach*

In Figures 4.5 and 4.6, the numbered dotted lines represent the prototype chains of the following objects:

c2/p2 ¬ Candidate.prototype ¬ Person.prototype ¬ Object.prototype ¬ null.

In the prototypal approach, 'pattern' replaces 'new', and there is no initialization for Person and Candidate.

4.6.2. *Summing up what we learned so far*

4.6.2.1. *Properties*

– Every object owns two types of properties: "*own*", or "*inherited*" by delegation from one prototype of its prototypes chain;

– among *own* properties, some are not enumerable: the property *[[prototype]]* is hidden, which protects it. Preserving the link, preserves the mechanism of delegation;

– the property constructor refers to the function f that provides its f.prototype to the object (if a literal f = Object). The constructor.name property is shared by all the objects of an equivalence class.

4.6.2.2. *Values*

– The value of a property is a reference: after deleting a property, the garbage collector will check if the referred value must be flushed or not.

4.6.2.3. *Methods*

– Methods are generally meant to be shared by the objects linked to the same prototype: you must add them to that prototype.

Methods defined in the constructor are "*static*" and methods defined in its prototype are "*delegated*". For example:

```
function Candidate(last, first){        // method in the constructor
    this.last = last; this.first = first;
    this.full = function(){return this.first+" "+this.last};
}
const c1 = new Candidate("Dupont"), c2 = new Candidate("Durand");
(c1.full === c2.full);                  // false: not shared
```

The full method is different for each new instruction. You may get hundreds!

```
function Candidate(last, first){
    this.last = last; this.first = first;
}                            // method in the prototype
Candidate.prototype.full = function(){return this.first+"..."};
(c1.full === c2.full);       // true: shared
```

A single method 'full' is delegated: not found among the own properties, the method is taken from the prototype. One unique version for hundreds!

4.6.2.4. Inheritance kinds (delegation, concatenation)

There are two ways to provide properties to an object:

– *delegation*: if the referred property is present in the prototypes chain, inheritance is dynamic. (see: 'Object.create');

– *concatenation*: if the referred property is copied from another object, it becomes static to be updated whenever necessary (see: 'Object.assign').

4.6.2.5 Multiple inheritance in JavaScript

An object inherits from only one prototype (*delegation*). The concatenation makes it possible to multiply static inheritances under the condition that the referred objects (from which copies are made) remain unchanged. This can be the case when we concatenate methods or specific values, which are meant to be constant. One solution can be to "freeze" those referred objects (Object.freeze), hence preserving them from later modifications.

4.6.2.6. Conclusion about the notion of "class" in JavaScript

There is no "class" nor "instance" in JavaScript, however we have learnt that a *generic concept* is provided by the "equivalence class" induced by the relation "has prototype", and we can name it (constructor.name). Any member of that class can be named an *"instance"*, if you are pleased with it.

5

Arrays

For a data scientist, handling arrays of tabulated data is a recurring task. The baseline, if using JavaScript, is to be able to do what we usually do with a spreadsheet and basic macrooperations. Thousands and thousands of tabulated data can be accessed freely on the Internet: public data for most countries, from international bodies, or free access private data. In Part 3, several applications will be discussed (e.g. French parliament election 2017).

JavaScript provides several built-in objects able to represent tabulated data, which we can access through an index. Array, of course, and TypedArray, Map, Set, String are other *"Iterables"*. They all share several features, such as the length property, but are named *"array-like"*. The list of arguments of a function, and a list of selected HTML DOM elements, are also *"array-like"* objects.

This chapter is devoted to the object "Array".

An *"array"* is a set of ordered values, which we can access with a numeric index. This index starts at 0 not 1 (*zero-based index*).

There is no specific type for arrays: the operator typeof returns "object", but the static method Array.isArray(tab) can check if its argument is an array, hence tab inherits all the Array.prototype methods.

5.1. Handling arrays: creation and access to its elements

5.1.1. *Creating an array with the array literal notation*

The syntax of an "array literal" uses [square brackets] to delimit a list of elements, which can be primitive values, variable names, objects and functions, separated by commas:

```
[elem1, elem2, ...] // any number of elements, including zero
```

Examples:

```
const tm = ["un", 2]; // two values: a string, a number
const ts = ["Jean","Bob"], tabn = [12,24]; // homogeneous arrays
const t2d = [ ts, tn];          // an array of two arrays
const te = [];                  // empty array: tab.length = 0
const tu = ["a",,"c"]; // syntactically correct, but to avoid!
```

WARNING.– When typing, do not remove an element, while leaving its comma: the array tu above has: tu.length = 3 and tu[1] = undefined.

Here are some best practices with arrays:

– declare an array with const: the elements, and their number, can be modified but it restricts the use of its name to that array, once for all;

– use the literal notation, not new Array(), it avoids ambiguities:

```
const tm = new Array("two"); // equiv: tm = ["two"];
const tn = new Array(2); // equiv.: tn = [undefined, undefined];
```

5.1.2. *Checking if a variable is an array*

The operator typeof does not distinguish an array from an object:

```
const t = [a, b, c]; console.log( typeof t ); // "object"
```

Instead, use the static method:

```
console.log( Array.isArray(t) ); // true
```

5.1.3. *The length property, the index count*

The length is in read–write access, and the index starts at 0 not 1:

```
console.log( [a, b, c].length );        // -> 3
const t = ["one", 2]; console.log( t[1]); // -> 2
```

The property length is permanently updated, returning the index of the last element plus one. Adding or removing an element in the array immediately modifies length. In turn, modifying length infers the addition or removal of elements, at or from the end of the array.

This feature can be used for some operations:

– *emptying an array: simply set length to zero*

```
const t1 = []; console.log(tab1.length); // -> 0 (t1 empty)
const t2 = ["one", "two", "three"];         // t2.length = 3
t2.length = 0; // now t2 is empty
```

The "garbage collector" will take care of the memory previously assigned to t2.

– *initializing an array to a given number of elements*

```
const t - []; t.length = N;       // [undefined, undefined,... N times]
```

NOTE.– An array is an object, with the specific ability to use numbers as property names, which is forbidden for a regular object:

```
const obj = {"p1":1, "p2":"two"};
console.log(obj["p2"]);      // two
console.log(obj[1]); // undefined (no such property)
```

NOTE.– We can add own properties to an array, as we do with objects. For example:

```
const t1 = [], t2 = [[], []];
// let's add the property 'dimension', then print values:
    t1.dimension = 1;        t2.dimension = 2;
console.log( t1["length"] +", "+ t1["dimension"] );     //-> 0, 1
console.log( t2["length"] +", "+ t2["dimension"] );     //-> 2, 2
```

5.1.4. *Accessing individual values in an array: the indices*

In the section `Array.prototype`, we will learn that it is often possible to avoid handling the individual elements of an array and rather work with the array as a whole. However, it is worth knowing how indices behave. Reminder: they start at zero.

```
const t = [2, 4];
let n = 1; console.log( t[n] ); // 4
n = 6; console.log( t[n] ); // undefined
n = -6; console.log( t[n] ); // undefined
```

The value `undefined` can result from either of the following cases:

– the index is out of bounds `[0, t.length-1]`;

– the index is correct, but the value actually is `undefined` ("missing value").

NOTE.– An index is an "object property name": the index is of type "`number`", but it is evaluated as a "`string`" when used for accessing an element, which is to say a "property" of the array:

```
( tab[1] === tab["1"] ); // -> true
```

NOTE.– Missing values: some methods ignore them, whereas a for loop enumerates them: e.g. `tu[1]` in the example `const tu = ["a", ,"c"]`; Recommendation: avoid unnecessary missing values.

5.2. Methods of the object Array and Array.prototype

By far, the best way to handle arrays is to use the `Array.prototype` methods and, whenever needed, the static methods of the object `Array`.

Methods	Description	Return
`Array.of()`	Initializes an array with the arguments	Array
`Array.from()`	Creates an array from an "*Iterable*"	Array
`Array.isArray()`	Checks if the argument is an "Array"	Boolean

Table 5.1. *The static methods of the object Array*

These static methods must be invoked from the built-in object `Array`. Example: `Array.isArray(["a","b"]);    // true`.

See section 5.2.5 for the use of `Array.from`.

By contrast, the methods of the object `Array.prototype` are delegated to every array. For example: `[].push("a");        // ["a"]`

The `Array.prototype` methods are grouped into three families: "Mutators", "Accessors" and "Iterators". We use the notation `[].method` to identify them.

5.2.1. The "Mutators" family

Nine methods that modify the array on which they are invoked; the array length may change. Several methods are useful at initialization stage:

– incremental insertion element by element ('push', 'unshift');

– copy a set of values ('fill', 'copyWithin');

– incremental removal of element by element ('pop', 'shift'),

– replacing a slice of values ('splice').

Methods	Description	Return
`a.copyWithin`	Moves a slice of the array according to *(target, start, end)*	tab
`a.fill`	Copies a same value according to *(val, start, end)*	tab
`a.pop` `a.shift`	*Removes the last (respectively, first) value, decrementing length*	valeur
`a.push` `a.unshift`	Adding a value at the end (respectively, beginning), incrementing length	length
`a.reverse`	Reverse the array	tab
`a.sort`	Alphabetical sort or according to comparator *(function)*	tab
`a.splice`	Modifies a slice according to *(start, count, [values list])*, modifies *length*	tab

Table 5.2. *"Mutators" methods of Array.prototype*

– The methods "fill", "push", "unshift"

– create an array of N identical values, for instance 0s:

```
const t = []; t.length = N;        t.fill(0);        // [0, 0, ... N]
```

– fill an array with values provided as a result of some requests:

```
let x; const t = [];    // start with an empty array
do{    x = Math.random() * (10 - 1) + 1;      // data in [1,10]
        if(x > 5){t.push(x.toFixed(1));}      // keep if > 5
} while (x > 5);                              // stop if ≤ 5
if(t.length > 0){t.unshift("random > 5");}        // set t[0] if t ≠ ∅
```

– The method "splice"

This makes it possible to "revise" an array by modifying one element or a slice. For instance, to update the first name of an object whose full name contains a given last name:

– line 1: sets the original array;

– line 2: selects with findIndex the element containing "Dent": gives k;

– line 3: uses splice to replace one value at index [k].

```
const t = ["Jean Bon", "Ange Leau", "P. Dent", "Paul Tron"];    //1
let k = t.findIndex(x=>x.includes("Dent")); // (see below)    //2
t.splice(k, 1, "Redon Dent"); // replaces the value for t[k]    //3
```

– The methods "reverse" and "sort"

These methods modify the order of the elements: "reverse" is trivial and "sort" is more complex.

```
const t = ["Jean Bon", "Ange Leau", "P. Dent", "Paul Tron"];
t.sort(); // ["Ange Leau", "Jean Bon", "P. Dent", "Paul Tron"]
```

– with no argument, "sort" makes a Unicode-based alphabetical sort;

– with a function 'compare' as argument, sort is made depending on the result of the compare function element by element:

```
function compare(a, b) {
    if (a < b [by some ordering criterion]) {return -1;}
    if (a > b [by same ordering criterion]) {return 1;}
    return 0; // because a = b
}
```

The function compare is used in a *quickSort* algorithm. The array is partitioned into slices, each slice having a pivot (value 'a'). At some point of the (ascending) sort, for each element (value 'b') preceding 'a', if compare(a,b) > 0, the element is moved, else left in place. A symmetric operation occurs if 'a' precedes 'b':

EXAMPLE 1.– Sorting is done by numbers (ascending order, ignoring Infinity, NaN)

```
function compareNumbers(a,b) {return a - b;}
[1, 4, 2, 11, 3].sort(compareNumbers);    // [1,2,3,4,11] (num)
[1, 4, 2, 11, 3].sort();                  // [1,11,2,3,4] (alpha!)
```

EXAMPLE 2.– Sorting is done by the last name in "first last" string.

```
function compareLastNames(a,b) {
        let al = a.split(" ")[1],    // second word in a
            bl = b.split(" ")[1];    // second word in b
        if (al < bl)           return -1;
        else if (al == bl)     return 0;
        else                   return 1;
}
const t = ["Jean Don","Ange Leau","P. Dent","Paul Tron"];
t.sort(compareLastNames);
                // ["Jean Bon","P. Dent","Ange Leau","Paul Tron"]
```

5.2.2. The "Accessors" family

Seven methods do not modify the array, but yield a representation of the data in the array, which can be a new array, an index value and a string.

Method	Description	Return
a.concat	Concatenates the array with the argument	Array
a.indexOf a.lastIndexOf	Index of the first/last occurrence of (*val*), or *-1* if not found	Number
a.slice	Copies a slice *(start,end)* into a new array	Array
a.join a.toLocaleString a.toString	Makes a string with all the values of the array similar to join (+"locale" format) similar to join (not choosing the separator)	String

Table 5.3. *"Accessors" methods of Array.prototype*

The use of these methods is rather straightforward.

5.2.3. The "Iteration" family

Repeat an operation for each element, not modifying the array. The result can be:

– a new array, same length (map), or shorter (filter);

– a selected value or index (find, findIndex);

– a cumulated value over the whole array (reduce, reduceRight);

– a plain iteration (forEach) of a block of operations element by element.

Method	Description	Return
a.entries a.keys a.values	Returns an array of couples *[key, value]* An array of *[key]* An array of *[value]*	*Iterator*
a.every a.some	Checks if all elements comply with *(function)* If one element complies *(function)*	Boolean
a.filter	Array of elements selected by *(function)*	Array
a.find a.findIndex	First value complying with *(function)*, or undefined index of that first value, or –1	Value Index
a.forEach	Processes *(function)* for each element	Undefined
a.map	New array with values modified according to *(function)*	Array
a.reduce a.reduceRigh	Cumulates the values according to *(function)* idem, from the end of the array	Value

Table 5.4. *"Iteration" methods of Array.prototype*

5.2.4. Iterating over the elements of an array

Important recommendations for handling arrays are as follows:

Use Array.prototype methods, not loops: it is easier and much less error prone.

There are two kinds of loops:

– *iteration* loop: 'for(let i = 0; i < t.length; i++)' or 'while..';

– *enumeration* loop: 'for(let prop in t)'.

The enumeration loop is not concerned by the remark. The iteration loop uses an index and the length of the array: we have pointed out the risks when declaring or forgetting-to-declare the index.

5.2.5. *Iteration without a loop, with Array/Array.prototype methods*

All basic operations for creating and handling arrays exist since ES6.

5.2.5.1. *Array.from*

This transforms an iterable into a regular array. For example:

```
const args = Array.from(arguments);      // within a function
const t2 = Array.from({length:3},function(){return 1}); // [1,1,1]
const t3 = Array.from({length:3},function(v,i){return i*i});
const t4 = Array.from("hello"); // ["h", "e", "l", "l", "o"]
const rd = Array.from({length:n},
                    function(x){return Math.random() * 10;});
```

- 'args': see section 6.3 (Chapter 6);

- 't2': identical to the example with "fill" (but in one instruction);

- 't3': the first argument {length:3} is an *iterable* (it has a length), it allows from to iterate the function (argument #2) three times to i*i: resulting in [0, 1, 4];

- 't4': transforms a string into an array;

- 'rd': a data series of n random numbers between 0 and 9.

5.2.5.2. *tab.forEach*

This runs the function for each element of the array tab. For example, to compute a value and at the same time, save some data in an additional array:

```
let rc = "figures ", rl = " and letters "; const tabc = [];
["a","b", 1, 2].forEach(function(v, i){
    if(typeof v === 'string') rl += (i===0?"" : ", ") + v;
    else tabc.push(v);
});
rc +tabc.toString()+ rl; // figures 1,2 and letters a, b
```

5.2.5.3. *tab.map*

This runs the function for each element of the array [], like forEach, plus saves the returned value into a new array. For example:

```
const tabl = ["a","b", 1, 2].map(function(v, i){
    return (typeof v === 'string'? v : v.toString());
});    // tabl will contain only 'strings'
```

5.2.5.4. *tab.every, tab.some*

This runs the function up to some element in the array. By contrast with most array methods, these methods can stop running before the end of the array:

– some: stops as soon as one element complies;

– every: stops as soon as one element does not comply

```
function isEven(elt, index, array) {return (elt % 2 == 0);}
[2,4,5,8,6,2,3,12,4,8,9,1].every(isEven);
                        // -> false (stops at '5')
[2,4,5,8,6,2,3,12,4,8,9,1].some(isEven);
                        // -> true (stops at first '2')
```

5.2.5.5. *tab.find, tab.findIndex:*

This stops as soon as the argument is found, and returns the value or the index.

```
function isPrime(v, i) {
        let f = 2;
        while (f <= Math.sqrt(v))
                {if (v % f++ < 1){return false;}}
        return v > 1;
}
[4, 5, 8, 12].findIndex(isPrime); //-> 1 (and stops)
```

5.2.5.6. *filter*

This selects the elements complying with the function into a new array. It is similar to the SQL command "Select_From_Where":

```
const upTo10 = Array.from({length:10},
        function(v,i){return i+1}); // [1,2,3,4,5,6,7,8,9,10]
const primes = upTo20.filter(isPrime);  // [2,3,5,7]
```

5.2.5.7. *reduce*

This aggregates onto an accumulator similarly to the SQL command "GroupBy":

```
function multAcc(acc, v){return acc *= v;}
const factorial = upTo10.reduce(multAcc);  // 3628800 (!)
```

Thanks to the polymorphism of +, we can aggregate onto a string:

```
function tPrim(acc, v){return acc +`(${v})`;}
const ini = "First primes: ";
const str = upTo10.filter(isPrime).reduce(tPrim,ini);
           // First primes: (2) (3) (5) (7)
```

Here reduce uses the second argument that initializes the accumulator:

```
["c1","c2"].reduce(function(s,x){s+`<li>${x}</li>`},"<p>")+"</p>";
// <p><li>c1</li><li>c2</li></p>
```

We will use this feature to create text to display on the web page (see Part 3). Another feature is used in that example: the chaining of methods.

5.2.6. *Chaining array methods*

This is a "*functional*" capacity provided by JavaScript: chaining methods means that the result of the first method is an object that accepts the next method. For example (above), the result of filter is an array, and we can invoke the method reduce on that array in a single instruction (over three lines for better readability):

```
Array.from({length:10}, function(v,i){return i+1})
      .filter(isPrime)
      .reduce(tPrim,ini);
```

With the help of the "arrow function syntax", you may even write:

```
Array.from({length:10}, (v,i)=>i+1)
      .filter(isPrime).reduce((s,p)=>s+`(${p})`,ini);
```

5.2.7. *Arrays and the arrow function syntax*

The arrow syntax can be used everywhere for function expressions, and in particular in the context of array methods, it may ease code readability, for example:

```
const f = function(x,i){do_something_with_x_and_i; return value;}
let out = tab.reduce(function(acc,x,i){return acc + f(x,i);},ini);
```

equivalent, in the arrow syntax , to:

```
const f = (x,i)=>{do_something_with_x_and_i; return value;}
let out = tab.reduce((acc,x,i)=>acc + f(x,i),ini);
```

Readability is improved if the code of the function is simply a short return instruction (e.g. 'out'). With a more complex code (e.g. function isPrime) the arrow syntax may not help much: you would rather put that code in a function to be called (e.g. similar to the f(x,i) above).

NOTE.– The arrow syntax introduces a difference in the handling of the pronoun this (which we will study later).

5.2.7.1. *Arguments of the callback functions in Array.prototype methods*

Most array methods accept a function as first argument (plus some optional arguments: see initial value of the accumulator, with reduce). This function argument accepts three arguments, or four, when used with reduce.

– Three arguments: for instance with `filter`

```
const t = Array.from({length:n}, ()=>Math.random()*10);
const tnew = t.filter(function(x, i, tbl){return /* code */});
// @x: is the current the element        // x: mandatory
// @i: is the current index (when required)
// @tbl: link to the array 't' (seldom useful)
```

NOTE.– t receives an array of n random numbers in the range [0–9].

– Four arguments, for instance with `reduce`

```
let str = t.reduce(function(acc, x,i,tbl){return acc+...;},acc0);
// @acc: is the accumulator, initialized to acc0 (if acc0 present)
//                            if no acc0, acc initialized to x[0]
// @x, i, tbl: as above// acc and x: mandatory
```

– Example: Data series transformed into %-change data series (**map+reduce**)

```
const t = Array.from({length:n}, ()=>Math.random()*10);
function pcentChange(x, i, tbl){return i>0? x - tbl[i-1]/x:0;}
// can be directly written into the map method,
// then chained with reduce to compute the mean average:
let mean =      t
                .map((x,i,tbl)=>i>0? x - tbl[i-1]/x:0;)
                .reduce((acc,x)=>acc+x) / t.length;
```

5.2.8. The "Iterables"

Several built-in objects have been added by ES6: `TypedArray`, `Map`, `Set` and an *"iterable"* behavior have been introduced in the norm, making them *"Iterable"* together with `String` and `Array`: all have a `length`, and know how to "iterate" on their elements, which allows `Array.from` to work.

`TypedArray`, `Map`, `Set` and `Array` all have their `forEach` method, and the DOM `NodeList` object as well (see Part 2).

The `Arguments` object, accessible within any function, under the name `arguments` is also an *Iterable*: `arguments.length` is ≥ 0 (not `undefined`) and we can make an array from it:

```
const args = Array.from(arguments)
```

5.3. Array of arrays (multidimensional array)

Handling multidimensional data (e.g. 2D) is a frequent task of the data scientist.

The "spreadsheet" is the most common pattern for simple databases (non-transactional DB). In many situations, these tabulated data are easy to collect and archive (very simple training). Each line of the file has a defined number of elements, and columns are "named", which can be easily translated into a JavaScript object notation:

```
const line_i = {"nameCol1": val1, "nameCol2": val2, ... };
```

Here is an example of a 2D array:

```
const t1 = [1, 2], t2 = [3, 4], t3 = [5, 6];
const tab2d = [t1, t2, t3];
              // tab2d[1][1] = 4          tab2d[2][0] = 5
              // tab2d[1]     = [3, 4]
console.log( tab2d );          //-> 1, 2, 3, 4, 5, 6
```

WARNING.– We should be aware of some traps:

– indices: the first index simulates the line, the second the column;

– sizes: tab2d.length gives the "number of lines", but for each array element the corresponding size may vary, and you must check if it is the correct "number of columns" (some frameworks do this for you). For example:

```
// let width=304, height=228 be the sizes of a picture
const t1 = [1, 2], t2 = [3, 4], t3 = [5, 6];
const tab2d = [t1, t2, t3];
tab2d.toString();       // 1,2,3,4,5,6
tab2d[1][2] = width;    // same as: t2[2] = width;
tab2d[1][3] = height;       // same as: t2[3] = height;
tab2d.toString();       // 1,2,3,4,304,228,5,6
// now, tab2d.length is still 3, t1.length = t3.length= 2,
// but t2.length= 4 (beware!)
```

EXAMPLE.– Extracting a single column from a 2D array:

```
let n = 1;       // warning: will refer the second column!
const col2 = tab2d.map(x => x[n] || null);
     // col2 = [2, 4, 6]
```

NOTE.– The shortcut "x[n] || null" is to avoid undefined, if cell n does not exist.

EXAMPLE.– Flattening a 2D array:

```
const tab1d = tab2d.reduce((acc,x) => acc.concat(x), []);
// tab1d = [1, 2, 3, 4, 5, 6]
```

NOTE.– acc is initialized to the empty array [] to which each line of tab2d is concatenated.

EXAMPLE.– Providing metadata to a 2D array:

An array is an object, with specific features (numbers as property names), and like an object, we can add properties besides .length; we can set a .title to name it, .dimension to inform about dimensionality, or .schemata, an array to name the columns of a 2D array, etc.

```
const t1 = [1, 2], t2 = [3, 4], t3 = [5, 6];
const tab2d = [t1, t2, t3];
tab2d.dimension = 2;
tab2d.schemata = ["date", "amount"];
tab2d.columnsOk = tab2d.every(x=>x.length === tab2d[0].length);
```

5.3.1. *Frameworks proposing an "augmented Array.prototype"*

There exists some stable and safe frameworks providing additional methods to arrays, though "masked" in their "namespace". For instance, statistical tools or LINQ-like queries ("Microsoft Language Integrated Query"), which you can find on GitHub, such as:

– jStat: https://github.com/jstat/jstat;

– jslinq: https://github.com/maurobussini/jsllnq.

6

Functions

A function is an independent block of code (instructions list), which can be called from another part of the code. This requires a mechanism for storing the calling line, sharing variables, passing parameters and returning a value.

In JavaScript, a function is a "first-class object", which means that a function can:

– be assigned to a variable;

– be an argument to other functions;

– be returned as a value;

– have properties, methods and a prototype, like every other object.

To illustrate this notion, we present a "prototypal diagram", as in Chapter 5, which shows how intricate "Object" and "Function" are:

```
Object.constructor =               Function
Object [[prototype]] ===           Function.prototype
Object.prototype.constructor =     Object
Object.prototype [[prototype]] === null              // alone
Function.constructor =             Function          // itself
Function [[prototype]] ===         Function.prototype
Function.prototype.constructor =   Function
Function.prototype [[prototype]] === Object.prototype
```

This chapter presents the notions of "*scope*" and "*execution context*", which will shed light upon the mechanisms of "*function closure*" and "*IIFE*" (immediately invoked function expression).

The diagram below summarizes what will be detailed, and where the notions of free variables and bound variables will be used.

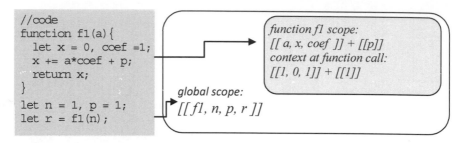

6.1. General syntax of a JavaScript function

A function can be set for the same syntax in two ways: by declaration or by expression.

```
function name([parameter1[, parameter2[, parameter3 ...]]])
{    /* code to be executed */
      [return value;] // optional, default: return undefined;
}
```

6.1.1. *Name*

The name of a function must not be a reserved word, nor be in conflict with the same name declared in the same "scope" (see the following). If no name is provided (only possible with a function expression), the function is called "*anonymous*"; if a name is provided, it is known inside the function and can be used for a recursive call.

6.1.2. *Parameters*

Parameters are identified by the operator parentheses (), not limited in number (script engine limit: 32766?). When the function is invoked, the values provided between parentheses, are called arguments and are matched with parameter names in the same order (see section 6.2).

NOTE.– Parameters are bound variables in the code block of the function; the arguments are passed by value only; their modification has no incidence outside the function.

6.1.3. *Return*

If there are explicit `return` statements, one must be the last statement of the block. If there is no explicit `return`, the value `undefined` is returned. Therefore, it is good practice to explicitly return a value, e.g. `return this;`

WARNING.– "Semicolon Insertion": a weird JavaScript feature with `return`:

```
return                          <- ; a semicolon is added here!
      "a_possibly_long_string";
```

The semicolon added at the end of the first line of the `return` causes ignorance of the following lines, and the function returns `undefined`.

6.1.4. *Function code block and scope*

The code block plays a particular role: this set of instructions forms what is called a *scope*. The declarations of variables or inner functions are added to this "*function scope*".

The "*hoisting*" mechanism described in Chapter 1 works inside the code block of the function: we strongly recommend again not to use `var`.

The variables that are not declared inside the block are sought into the scope of the instruction from which the function has been invoked, or, if not found, are seeked recursively up to the "*global scope*" ('window' if we are in the ecosystem of the web page).

6.1.5. Creating functions

There are two ways to build a function: declaration or expression.

– Function declaration

```
function add(a,b){ let c = a+b; return c; }
```

In this, the name of the function is mandatory. Due to the "hoisting", declared functions are grouped at the head of the code block that contains them. The code block of these functions may in turn contain function declarations and "hoisting" applies again, and so on (see section 6.5).

NOTE.– The function declaration instruction ends with a closing curly brace, which closes the code block. Do not add a semicolon after that (more recognizable).

– *Function expression*

```
const add = function(a,b){let c = a+b; return c;};      //case 1
```

The function expression (right-hand side) is assigned to a variable (left-hand side) that becomes the name of that function, and its type is function. Use const to declare the variable that receives the function expression.

NOTE.– The semicolon that terminates the instruction.

A function expression can be found in two more situations:

– defining the method of an object (case 2),

```
const personne = {
      nom: "Dupont", prenom: "Jean",
      affiche(){return this.prenom +" "+ this.nom;}      //case 2
      };
```

– defining the value of an argument of another function (case 3):

```
["Jo","Bob","Ron"].forEach(function(x){emailTo(x);});    //case 3
```

The name of the function is optional with a function expression, since ES6 the name of the variable (case 1) or the key of the method (case 2) is given as a name to the function. Only in case 3, the unnamed function used as argument remains really anonymous. But even then, you can always use an explicit name.

6.2. Invoking a function with operator (.)

The operator (parentheses), also called "grouping operator" or "precedence operator", is used in arithmetic or logic expressions or regular expressions. It tells the engine to process the parenthesized parts first, thus establishing a precedence on what the parentheses operator groups.

6.2.1. *The three facets of the "parentheses operator" in a function context*

– Parameters delimiter

This is used in function declaration syntax, after the name, or in an anonymous function expression.

```
function test ( p1, p2 ) { ... }
function Candidate ( first, last ) { ... }
[1,2].forEach(function ( x, i ) { ... });
```

– Arguments delimiter

This is used with a declared function that is invoked in an instruction, either as a direct call, or with operator new. In both cases, the list of arguments, possibly empty, will be matched with the list of the expected parameters.

```
test ( "hello" );                       // matches p1, p2 undefined
const = new Candidate ( "Jean", "Dupont" ); // matches ...
```

– Immediate invocation see section 6.7 ("IIFE")

When used to parenthesize a full function syntax, its effect is to tell the engine to process that function first, which means to execute its code, using a mandatory second pair of parentheses that must contain the arguments, possibly none.

```
( function (x,i){ ... } ) ( "hello",12 );
                          // "hello" matches x, 12 matches i
```

Let us detail the three steps of the "argument delimiter" situation:

– Matching arguments to parameters:

JavaScript accepts that numbers be different: same rank items are matched, parameters in excess are set undefined, arguments in excess are ignored.

– Function execution:

The function name gives access to the code, which is executed with the matched parameters, and with the values of the variables that are present in the "execution context" provided by the calling instruction (see below).

– Return. There is always a returned value:

Either the evaluated expression from the instruction return (expression); or the object (when using new), or undefined, by default.

WARNING.– Execution context. This is unambiguous for the script engine, but it could be so for you, because the context is dynamic. See sections 6.5.1.1 (scope), 6.5.4 ("boundThis") and 6.6 ("closure") for a comprehensive evaluation of this (sometimes) difficult issue.

WARNING.– Return value. Though we do not recommend to use new, it may be necessary sometimes (using existing code, etc.). Thus, we recommend to add a "return this;" statement, whenever there is no explicit return in the code.

6.3. *Choosing function declaration versus function expression*

Let us compare three examples.

– *Using function declaration:*

```
let x = add(4, 3); // the value of 'return' is assigned to x
function add(a, b) { let c = a+b; return c; }
console.log(x); // -> 7 Ok!
```

The function add is hoisted before x.

– *Using a variable and an anonymous function expression:*

```
let x = add(4,3);
const add = function (a, b) { let c = a+b; return c; };
// ReferenceError: can't access lexical declaration `add' before
initialization
```

The function add is not hoisted and defined later than x.

– Using a variable and a named function expression:

```
const add = function adding(a, b) { let c = a+b; return c; };
let x = adding(4,3);
// ReferenceError: adding is not defined
```

The name `adding` is only known inside the function →   *Beware!*

– Differences:

– the "*hoisting*" works only on function declarations;

– the function expression becomes the value of the variable: only the name of this variable is known outside the function. Inside the function, the name to use is `adding` though both `add` and `adding` are known (but `add` refers `adding`).

These differences concern only the scope of the names, with no consequence on the execution of the function. Choosing between function declaration and function expression is therefore just a matter of coding style.

6.4. Arguments

The parameters are declared together with the function; the arguments are passed when function is invoked.

6.4.1. *The arguments are passed by value*

The function may modify, in its code block, the value corresponding to an argument, but the corresponding variable outside the function is not affected: it is the value of the matched parameter not of the variable.

WARNING.– An object passed in argument is not modified, but its properties may be modified, even deleted, and new ones may have been added by the function. The same remark applies for arrays. A container whose content changes is still the same unchanged container.

Code	Value of: **x.first**		
	(before)	inside	(after)
`let x = {"first": "Victor"}`	*Victor*		
`function changeObject(x)` `{x = {first:"Julia"};}`	*Victor*	*Julia*	*Victor*
`function changeMember(x)` `{x.first = "Julia";}`	*Victor*	*Julia*	*Julia*

Table 6.1. *Changing the contents or the container*

6.4.2. *The inner object "arguments"*

Each function has access to an inner object arguments, which is the list of the values that are received as arguments at invocation time. This is an "Iterable" that we can handle with Array.from(arguments).

EXAMPLE.– List the actual arguments, even not expected as parameters

```
function f(){          // no parameter expected
   Array.from(arguments).forEach( a=>{console.log(typeof a);} );
}
f("1", 2, "hello"); // -> string number string
```

6.5. Scope: global scope, function scopes and block scopes

Here is another fundamental facet of JavaScript, whose understanding is key to writing correct, robust and reusable code.

6.5.1. *Vocabulary: lexical scope and "namespace"*

Every variable or function must be declared and named somehow:

– variable: using keywords ~~var~~, let or const followed by a name;

– function: using the keyword function, followed by a name, or, indirectly, by assigning a function expression to a variable, declared as above.

6.5.1.1. *Scope*

The scope of a variable or a function is the set of instructions where its name is lexically known, not provoking a ReferenceError exception. This set of instructions, which we can associate to a scope, can be delimited by {"curly braces"} in only two ways:

– "*function scope*": in the code block of a function;

– "*block scope*": the variable declared by let or const are lexically bound to one existing block, like a conditional branch or loop, or an explicit {"curly braces delimited block"};

– else: the variable is global, the *global scope* is not delimited.

6.5.1.2. *Namespace*

The term "*namespace*" may be linked to "*scope*" by metonymy. Indeed a "*namespace*" is an object, whose own properties and methods are those of a scope (maybe with some private additions). One example is to relate the "*window namespace*" and the *global scope*, when JavaScript is run into the web page ecosystem. In that case, the global variable a is exactly the property window.a.

See Chapter 7, the design pattern for creating a "namespace".

6.5.1.3. *Breaking down variables and functions by scope*

The code of this example is merely written for learning purposes: to create several scopes (see Figure 6.1)

```
function f1(b){
   const coef = 4;
   if(b >8 && b < 10){let str = "(before extra time) "; a += str;}
   return a + coef * b;
}
function f2(){
   let y = 3;
   fff = function f3(y){
      const z = 3, str = ". You have played "+(z-y)+" times";
      if(y > 0){ y-; f3(y);}
      return str;
   };
   return fff(y);
```

```
}
let a = "Your score is: ",
    b = 12,
    str = "Result. "+ f1(a, b) + f2();console.log( str );
```

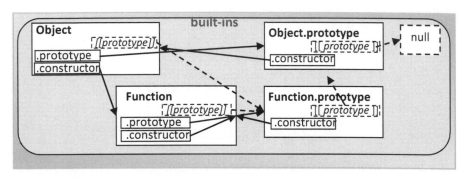

Figure.6.1. *Intrication of the "Object" and "Function" built_in object*

6.5.1.4. *Explanation: free variables versus bound variables*

In mathematics, the notions of *"free variables"* and *"bound variables"* are meant to tell if we can reuse them or not in a compound proposition. In the present discussion, when a scope provides the list of variables that are declared in it, this is its list of *[[bound variables]]*. If more variables are present, but not listed, then they are "free". We must seek one other scope in which they are "bound": first, in the scope of the calling instruction, then up again until we found this scope, which can be the "global scope". Finally, if not found at all, this search yields a Reference Error exception.

Let us break down our example, scope by scope:

– global scope = [[f1, f2, a, b, str]]: two functions and three variables;

– function scope f1 = [[b, coef]]: one local variable, one parameter;

WARNING.– The invocation f1 (b) uses the global variable b, whose value is passed as argument, and becomes the value of the parameter b, same name but this b is local to f1. These are distinct variables: if f1 modifies b, the global b is unchanged!

– bloc scope if in f1 = [[str]] + *global?[[a]]*

The variable str is local to the block (declared with let). The variable a used in the block is not local, nor local in function f1. We find a in the global scope, and we use it. We must browse the whole *scope chain* to find the right variable.

– function scope f2 = [[y, fff]]: two local variables, no parameters;

– function scope fff = [[f3, y, z, str]]

The function referred to by fff is not anonymous, but named f3 (inner name). This name is unknown to f2 because the function expression is assigned to fff only name bound to f2. There is one parameter y, which, for reasons already explained, is local to fff, totally unrelated to the y of f2. Two more variables are locally bound, z and str; this name already in use in a different scope, which doesn't cause any problem.

6.5.1.5. *The "scope chain"*

Reading the lexical tree helps in setting the *scope chain* for each variable or function. At run-time, a variable is either *bound*, and we can fetch it value, or *"free"* and we must browse the *scope chain* to fetch its value. Example: a in the if-block of function f1, is bound to global scope.

The scope chain is oriented upwards: one level can access its bound variables and those of the upper levels, but without access to lower levels.

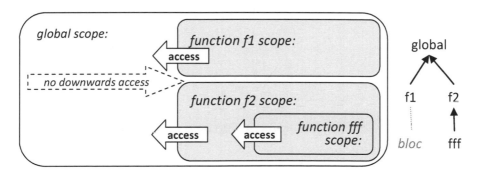

Figure 6.2. *The scope chain is oriented upwards*

The propagation of modifications is downwards oriented: modifying a variable at some level may impact only lower levels. Example: the variable a, bound to the global scope, brings its value at f1, but modifying str in function fff has no impact on the global variable str.

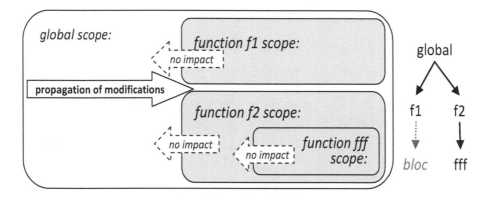

Figure 6.3. *Value modifications propagate downwards*

6.5.2. *Wrapping-up and warnings*

Within a same scope:

– all function declarations are hoisted within their scope, at lexical time;

– all let and const declarations are "lexically" part of their scope, but cannot be referenced before being initialized (ReferenceError);

– a same name cannot be re-declared in the same scope (SyntaxError).

WARNING.– Items 2 and 3 above, do not apply to var declarations, and you must remember that with var declarations: (a) the variables are hoisted within a function or global scope, not within a block; (b) inner functions are hoisted first; (c) name redeclarations are silently accepted, and surprises may come later:

```
var g = 0;
function g(){}
console.log(typeof g);  // "string" (g: not a function!)
```

6.5.2.1. *Conclusion*

We must remember the following: (see also: sections "closure", "IIFE")

– the propagation of modifications is never ascending, therefore, creating an inner scope will protect your code against unwanted conflicts;

– the only way to access a variable from a lower level function block is through a return mechanism. Use an object if you have to regroup several values.

We are sometimes in the situation of reusing some code, and integrating it into a larger application code. This can be painful, in general because of unnoticed scope conflicts, in particular if this code has been written before ES6. Here are some recommendations, which may help:

– first, replace all var with const;

– at lexical time, you may get several "**SyntaxError: redeclaration..**", which are easy to correct, and insures you against involuntary name repetitions in a same scope;

– you may get "**SyntaxError: missing = in const declaration**", and you have to decide either to initialize the variable, or to use let instead;

– at run-time, you may get "**TypeError: invalid assignment to const**" which will be easily corrected, probably replacing const with let;

Finally, here is a series of short exercises that should convince you that using var is definitely the last thing to do.

6.5.2.2. *Comments about the harmfulness of 'var'*

After each exercise, change var to const (or let).

```
#1. Yes or No?
var response = function() {return "Yes";};
function response() {return "No";}
console.log( response() );        // -> ?
```

#2. A small omission may make a big difference:
```
var carName = "Rolls"; // global
function aFunction(x, y) { var carName = "Clio"; x += y; }
aFunction(10, 2);
console.log("my car is a "+ carName); // -> ?
  compare with: (#2.bis)
function aFunction(x, y) { carName = "Clio"; x += y; }
aFunction(10, 2);
console.log("my car is a "+ carName); // -> ?
```

#3. A small difference may make a big difference:
```
var num1 = 1, num2 = 3, nom = "Maradona";
function f1() { return num1 * num2; }
function getScore () {
  var num1 = 1, num2 = 20;
  function f2() { return nom + " scored " + f1() +" buts"; }
  return f2();
}
console.log( getScore() ); // what is the #3 result?
  compare with: (#3.bis)   (there are lures and traps to avoid ...!)
function getScore () {
  var num1 = 1; num2 = 20;
  function f2() { return nom + " scored " + f1() +" goals"; }
  return f2();
}
console.log( getScore() ); // what is the #3bis result?
```

#4. Explain why this code returns that result, then try let.
```
function f2(cond){
  var g = 0;
  if (cond) { function g() { return "blabla"; } }
  return typeof g +", ";
}
console.log( f2(true) + f2() )// result: "function, number, "
```

Table 6.2. *Series of exercises to get rid of 'var'*

Will you still use var, after that?

6.5.2.3. *Comments about the inner mechanism of a function*

Every function owns several visible properties, we already know prototype, and name, and also some hidden ones, not part of the norm, but which the engine knows. We already know *[[prototype]]*, and we know that it is not the same as prototype. Here are some more properties.

Property	Value description
Name	Name of the function: a string
Prototype	Refer the "companion" object of every function
[[prototype]]	Like every object
[[Call]]	Used when the function is invoked by simple call ()
[[Code]]	Code text between { }
[[FormalParameters]]	The list of parameters to be matched with the "arguments" object when the function is invoked
[[BoundThis]]	The value of pronoun this to refer the calling object
[[Scope]]	"Scope chain". Used with "closures"
[[Construct]]	Used when invoked by 'new', to build the "prototype"

Table 6.3. *Some properties of functions*[1]

Without getting into details, it may help to know that the script engine, when a function is invoked, must have access to the scope chain of the variables (to distinguish between free and bound), to the value of the arguments, to the value of the pronoun this and to the calling context. The global object owns a hidden property, the object *[[Stack]]* that implements the invocation chain and provides the calling context: where to go back from g, if f invokes g, etc.

6.6. Function "closures"

We can nest functions in JavaScript and communications work this way:

– an inner function can receive values through the arguments passed from the calling function to the inner function;

– an inner function has access to the bound and free variables of the calling function, and recursively up to global variables;

– the calling function has no access to the bound variables of an inner function, and can only receive a value through a return statement.

---

1 Excerpt from https://danmartensen.svbtle.com/the-anatomy-of-a-javascript-function.

Because functions are *first-class objects,* a function can be sent back by a return statement. And this is called a *"function closure"*, which means that you enclose the code of a function, together with a copy of the state of free variables, at the time when the closure is created and sent (a kind of frozen value).

As quoted by Kyle Simpson:

"Closure is when a function can remember and access its lexical scope even when it's invoked outside its lexical scope" (https://github.com/ getify/You-Dont-Know-JS).

Let us study this mechanism with a series of examples, which, moreover, can be used as programming *"design patterns"*.

6.6.1. *Saving the value of a free variable in a given context*

The goal is to save a context (at least one variable), and access it later, while ensuring it has not been modified during that interval.

The example of a counter:

```
let i = 0, nom = "A";          // initializes a global variable
function inc(){i++; return "nom"+i;}    // incrementation
```

This function increments i but so may other instructions: let us protect i by a closure:

```
function countFab(nom) {       // if we want to name the counter
      let i = 0;          // initialized once, when closure is created
      return function () { i++; return nom+":"+i; }
}
const counterA = countFab("A"); // counter "A" (i=0)
counterA();                            // A:1
counterA();                            // A:2
```

The same closure can be used to create several independent counters:

```
const counterB = countFab("B");        // counter "B" (and its own i)
counterA();    counterB();             // A:3, B:1
counterA();    counterB();             // A:4, B:2
```

The question is often asked: How can we write a closure from a regular function? The answer is the algorithm provided in Figure 6.5.

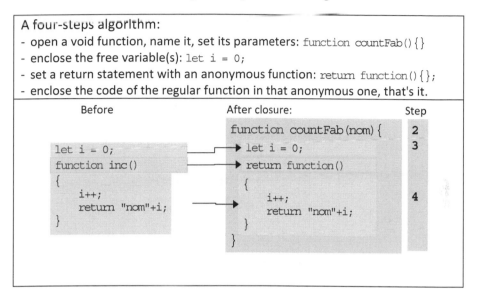

Figure 6.4. *The 4-step algorithm to build a closure*

The closure returns the targeted regular function: now you must save one copy in a given variable: const counterA = countFab("A");

NOTE.– The global variable i just disappeared; it has been "enclosed".

6.6.2. *Creating a list of functions linked to an array of data*

EXAMPLE.– Build a list of functions according to a list of languages (en, fr, cn ...).

This example will be studied thoroughly, as it is the archetype of the issues raised when scope and execution contexts are mixed up. We keep the var declaration first in order to demonstrate how tricky it was to code JavaScript before ES6.

We need a helper function print to display some intermediate values in order to clearly understand what is going on: print(s) should print s + (a list of results).

```
function print(s){
    return lgs.reduce((acc,x,i)=>acc+` cas${i}:${fns[i]()}`,s);
}
const lgs = ["fr","en","cn"],   // a list of languages
      fns = [];          // the array to fill in with functions
```

Every fns[i] must produce a string marking which language is used:
fns[i] = function(){ return "L["+ i +":"+ lgs[i] +"]"; };

The expected result when calling print("expected:") is:

```
// expected: cas0:L[0:fr] cas1:L[1:en] cas2:L[2:cn]
```

6.6.2.1. *First attempt: using a for-loop (and old-style 'var' declaration)*

```
for (var i = 0; i < lgs.length; i++) {
    fns[i] = function() { return "L["+ i +":"+ lgs[i] +"]"; };
}
console.log( print("Var") );
//Var: cas0:L[3:undefined] cas1:L[3:undefined] cas2:L[3:undefined]
```

Disappointing result!

The i=3 and lgs[i]=undefined comes from each fns[i] in all cases. But the index for casN, coming from function print, increments correctly.

Why?

Because the value of i when executing a fns, is its value in print(), hence after the end of the loop, and that value is lgs.length (stop condition) which means i=3 and lgs[i]=undefined. The value of i at the creation of fns[i] has been erased. On the other side, the index i used in print is local to that function.

6.6.2.2. *Second attempt: using a "closure"*

Let us apply the algorithm that we have just learned:

– begin with: const clo = function(i){...}, the free variable is the parameter i, so step 2 is done as well;

– add the return of an anonymous function:

```
const clo = function(i){return function(){...};};
```

– add the code in that anonymous function:

```
const clo = function(i){return function(){
                        return `L[${i}:${lgs[i]}]`;};};
```

NOTE.– The inner i has been saved at the creation of the closure.

– finally, let us introduce the closure in the main loop to create the fns:

```
for (var i = 0; i < lgs.length; i++) {
    const clo = function(i){return function(){
                        return `L[${i}:${lgs[i]}]`;};};
    fns[i] = clo(i);
}
console.log( print("Clo:") );
// Clo: cas0:L[0:fr] cas1:L[1:en] cas2:L[2:cn]                Eureka!
```

RESULT.– The closure, called three times, saved three original values of its argument i, QED (*Quod Erat Demonstrandum*).

You may imagine that this issue has already been faced by thousands of programmers before us. It was one motivation for introducing the declaration 'let' in ES6.

6.6.2.3. *Third attempt: using the declaration 'let' in the loop*

```
const fns = [];
for (let i = 0; i < lgs.length; i++) {  // let i
    fns[i] = function() { return "L["+ i +":"+ lgs[i] +"]";};
}
print("Let:"); // Let: cas0:L[0:fr] cas1:L[1:en] cas2:L[2:cn]
```

The inner implementation of let indeed executes a closure.

6.6.2.4. *Fourth attempt: remove the loop, use Array.prototype.map*

```
const fns = lgs.map( function(x,i) {
    return function(){return "L[" + i +":"+ x +"]";};
});
print("Map:"); // Map: cas0:L[0:fr] cas1:L[1:en] cas2:L[2:cn]
```

Removing the loop has many advantages: shorter, clearer and it is correct.

6.6.2.5. *Fifth attempt: for fun, the arrow version, the shorter one*

With the formatting solution adopted with the other "attempts".

```
const fns = lgs.map((x,i) => ()=>`L[${i}:${x}]`);
```

6.6.3. *"Currying": breaking down a function into 1-parameter functions*

Given a function with two parameters f(a,b), we know how to save one argument with a closure, as we did for a free variable, and pass the second to a new 1-parameter function.

EXAMPLE.– To say "hello" or "bonjour", depending on a given language, to a given person's name.

```
function salute(lg, last) { // regular version
   let str = (lg==='fr')?"Bonjour ":"Hello ";
   return str + last;
}
salute("en", "Peter");      //-> Hello Peter
salute("fr", "Pierre");     //-> Bonjour Pierre
```

One closure memorizes the chosen language:

```
function saluteIn(lg) {// closure version
   let name = (lg==='fr')?"Bonjour ":"Hello ";
   return function(nom){ return name + nom; }
}
const hello = saluteIn("en");      // memorises "en"
const bonjour = saluteIn("fr");    // memorises "fr"
hello("Peter");         // -> Hello Peter
bonjour("Pierre");      // -> Bonjour Pierre
```

The 1-parameter function saluteIn allows us to create two new functions memorizing two different states. If those functions have more than one parameter, the same mechanism can be applied, until we have a sequence of only 1-parameter functions. This global operation is called "currying", after Haskell Curry (*"functional programming"*).

JavaScript demonstrates its functional facet:

```
saluteIn("fr")("Pierre");   //-> Bonjour Pierre
saluteIn("en")("Peter");    //-> Hello Peter
```

```
|-------|-----|--------|
|-------| arg1 |        | -> invocation 1: save arg1

    closure     arg2    -> invocation 2: result with arg2
```

The usual example of currying is this one (to add several numbers):

– regular version with three parameters:

```
function regulAdd(a, b, c){return a+b+c;}
```

– curried version:

```
function curryAdd(a){return function(b){return function(c){return a+b+c;}}};
```

– curry-arrowed version:

```
const curryarrowAdd = a=> b=> c=> a+b+c;
```

– verification:

```
curryAdd("a")("b")("c") === regulAdd("a", "b", "c"); // abc===abc
```

6.6.4. *Compositing functions from an array of functions*

For the curious, the amateur of sensation or just for fun: here we start with functional programming (an example from Eric Elliott). The following statement uses two ES6 innovations: the "arrow functions" and the "spread operator", but beyond these "elliptical" syntax elements, the important aspect is the pure functional use of JavaScript:

```
const pipe = (...fs) => x => fs.reduce((y, f) => f(y), x);
```

EXPLANATION.–

The "arrow" syntax compounds three parts: the (parameters list), the arrow and the code block. Example:

```
const f = function(x,y,z){return x+y+z;}      // regular syntax
const f = (x,y,z) => x+y+z;                    // "arrow" syntax
```

The "rest" syntax creates an array from a list, for example:

```
function f(...list) {return "array size "+list.length;}
f(1,3,5,7);    //-> array size = 4   [only known at run-time]
```

Now, we can start analyzing the mysterious function pipe:

– the innermost: fs.reduce((y,f)=> f(y), x);

– translates   fs.reduce(function(y,f){return f(y);},x);

– the part: x => fs.reduce((y,f)=> f(y), x);

– translates   function(x){return fs.reduce(function(y,f){return f(y);}, x);};

– fs is an array of functions and x is a function, the reduce method does the following:

– step1: y= x, f= f1, resulting in: y= f1(x);

– step2: y= f1(x), f= f2, resulting in: y= f2(f1(x)), ...

This is the functional magic of JavaScript: each function is composed of the result of the previous composition. To be applied to the list (...fs), the constraint is that these functions be "composable".

Here is the pipe version:

```
const toLower = s => s.toLowerCase(), // composable version
     httpize = s => `http://${s}.uno`,
     toEverybody = pipe(toLower, httpize, encodeURIComponent);
toEverybody("HelloWorld");
```

The equivalent explicit composition is:

```
encodeURIComponent( httpize( toLower("HelloWorld") ));
```

both versions resulting in:

```
HelloWorld → helloworld → http://helloworld.uno →
http%3A%2F%2Fhelloworld.uno
```

The interest of the pipe version is that the list of functions can be dynamically determined at run-time.

6.7. Immediately invocable functions: IIFE

Let us take again the example, with the declaration then the call of the closure:

```
function saluteIn(lg) {
    let str = (lg==='fr')?"Bonjour ":"Hello ";
    return function(nom) { return str + nom; }
}
const hello = saluteIn("en");   // memorises "en"
```

The mechanism of IIFE provides an elegant solution for combining these two instructions into one by anonymizing the function saluteIn.

```
const hello = ( function (lg) {
    let str = (lg==='fr')?"Bonjour ":"Hello ";
    return function(nom) { return str + nom; }
} )("en");      // memorises "en"
```

EXPLANATION.–

Parentheses (shown in bold font) stand for the "precedence operator", which means that the expression between (.) is evaluated first, and, because it is a function expression, the result is code, stored in memory *[[f]]*, then invoked by the second pair of parentheses, interpreted here as a "grouping operator" containing the arguments, and executed immediately:

```
( function(lg){ ...} ) → [[f]], then: const hello = [[f]]( "en" );
```

NOTE.– Be aware of the succession of parentheses: pair 1 = creation of the anonymous function; pair 2 = invocation with arguments, which are matched with the parameters of the anonymous function.

The example with saluteIn shows that, if you have to re-use the function, it is preferable to store it explicitly within a variable, which uses less resources than two IIFEs. Hence an IIFE is rather useful with single use cases.

6.7.1. Creating a "namespace", or a named library, with an IIFE

Creating a "*namespace*" is a popular single use case for an IIFE: first, create a "function scope", to avoid any conflict with the rest of the code:

```
( function (window, undefined) {
    // set of private functions and variables
} ) (window, undefined);
```

Passing to the IIFE the values of usual global variables, such as 'window', 'undefined', makes them "local" to the IIFE: this may provide a performance gain because they will be locally "resolved".

Assigning that IIFE to a variable gives the inner functions and variables a "prefix", which "names" this "space" of variable:

```
const nameSpaceA = (function(window, document, undefined) {
    // code -> build an object objA
        return objA;                 // return that object
}) (window, document, undefined);
```

Thus, any method or property of this object, immediately created and returned by the IIFE, will be accessible by:

```
let p = nameSpaceA.property;
let s = nameSpaceA.method();
```

This programming pattern is detailed in Chapter 7.

6.8. The methods of Function.prototype

These three methods are all meant to modify the context in which the function is applied by linking a given object with the inner pronoun "this".

Method	Description	Action
f.apply	Invokes f with a given this, and an array-like *(this, array)*	exec
f.call	invokes f with a given this, and a list of arguments *(this, arg1, ...)*	exec
f.bind	Clones f with a given this, and a list of arguments *(this, arg1, ...)*	returns a new function

Think of this sentence: "*no, not him, ... him!*", have you never said that?

It is sometimes necessary to invoke a function in a context different from its regular default context: the pronoun this always has the value of an object, whose properties can be used or modified. A specific section details the behavior of this pronoun (see Chapter 7). For now, let's say that the most frequent value for this pronoun is the global object, and we know that a function invoked with new creates a new object, thus assigning this to that object.

To force the modification of this is called a "binding". A binding is necessary, in particular when handling an array, to have this referring that array.

In Chapter 4 "Objects", we have seen use cases:

```
Candidate.prototype.fullName = function(){
    return Person.prototype.fullName.call(this)+", at "+this.dN;
};
```

the method Person.fullname is recycled as part of the expression for the corresponding Candidate.fullname method.

The introduction of new array methods in ES6, has also brought a way to bind this, directly from one optional parameter, and making the binding easier in some situations, for instance (contrived example):

```
const arr1 = [1, 2, 3];
const arr2 = ["a", "b", "c"];
const f = function(x,i,a){return `${i>0?a[i-1]:"0"} to ${x} - ${this[i]}`};
        // a will refer 'arr1'
const arr3 = arr1.map(f, arr2));        // this will refer 'arr2'
// "0 to 1 = a", "1 to 2 = b", "2 to 3 = c"]
```

In this way, we can use two arrays in the function.

The introduction of the Array.from method by ES6 has eliminated countless calls to slice.call, such as:

```
var nodes = Array.prototype.slice.call(nodeList);     // pre ES6
const nodes = Array.from(nodeList);                    // post ES6
```

6.8.1. *Function.prototype.call() and .apply(), and pronoun 'this'*

In the previous example, the target function is `slice` and the object to which bind `this` is always the first argument, followed by the usual arguments of the target function (in same order and number!): no one for that use of `slice`. Result: the binding allows `nodeList` to be passed to function `slice`.

The methods `call` and `apply` do not modify the function, they just bind the pronoun `this`. The difference is in the way the arguments (after the first one) are passed: as a list or as an array:

```
function f(arg1, arg2, arg3){...}
f.call(scope, arg1, arg2, arg3)      // list of individual arguments
f.apply(scope, [arg1, arg2, arg3])   // one argument Array
```

6.8.2. *Function.prototype.bind()*

The method `bind` does not *invoke* the function but returns one, which can be passed as argument, and whose `this` is bound to a given object (let us name it `scope`). This is an indirect way to "pass" an object, though we cannot pass it as an argument, for instance when using "callback" functions (very useful when handling HTML DOM elements):

```
function toggNav(evt){}// callback for a "DOM event"
nav.addEventListener('click', toggNav);
```

Such a callback function has some parameters (`evt`) constrained by the HTML DOM interface (see Part 2). How to pass `toggNav` a given object?

```
nav.addEventListener('click', toggleNav(scope)); // NO!!
```

Frequent 'novice' error: it does not pass the function but a return result.

One way is to write an anonymous function, with the API parameters, and use free variables (but you know, free variables are risky):

```
nav.addEventListener('click', function(evt){toggNav(scope);});
```

This next solution, using bind, creates a function whose this is bound to scope, while keeping the API required arguments (evt) for toggNav:

```
nav.addEventListener('click', toggNav.bind(scope, evt));
```

WARNING.– The bound function has the code of the target, with pronoun this modified once and permanently. To not forget, you should rather write:

```
const boundToggNav = toggNav.bind(scope, evt);
nav.addEventListener('click', boundToggNav);
```

6.9. Built-in functions

JavaScript provides a few top-level predefined functions:

– isFinite and isNaN   (see chapter 3 "numbers");

– parseInt, parseFloat   (idem);

– eval   (recommendation: do not use);

– encodeURI, decodeURI, encodeURIComponent, decodeURIComponent (URI formatting helpers);

– Number and String, when not invoked with the operator new, can be useful with an object Date, for instance:

```
let d = new Date ("December 17, 1995 03:24:00")
console.log ( Number(d) ) ;          // 819167040000
  // milliseconds since 01 January, 1970 UTC, negative before
String(new Date(0));                 // Thu Jan 01 1970 01:00:00 GMT+01
String(new Date(819167040000));      // Sun Dec 17 1995 03:24:00 GMT+01
```

6.10. Closure and IIFE cheat-sheet

Three ways to code a counter: (1) incrementing a free variable from the global context, (2) save a bound variable in a closure and increment that inner variable, and (3) the IIFE version of (2).

– With a global variable:

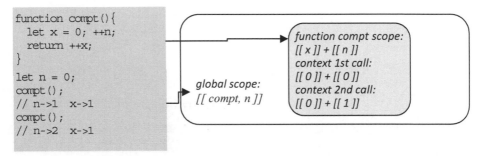

– With a closure (no global variable):

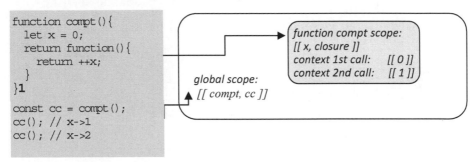

– Idem (IIFE version):

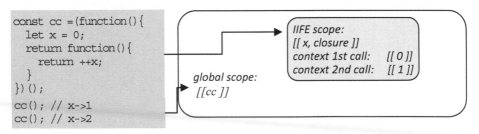

EXPLANATIONS.–

1) The bound variable x of compt is initialized at 0 at first call, then incremented. At next call, x is initialized again: the result is incorrect. The free variable n is incremented correctly, but it is a global variable.

2) The bound variable x is initialized at 0 when creating the closure cc = compt(); Then cc() invokes the inner function that increments x. So do next calls. Modifying x can be done solely within the closure: the variable is private.

3) Same mechanism as (2), performed immediately with the evaluation of the IIFE.

From Signs to Patterns

This chapter gathers several notions about the signs and words used in JavaScript, how they interact with the syntax (the traps of polymorphism), how to use programming constraints to style a more readable and robust code and a few hints about meta-programming.

In any language, punctuation plays a role in the interpretation. It is reported in 1327 that Queen Isabella signed the following order about her husband, Edward II:

```
Edwardum occidere nolite        // "do not execute Edward"
timere bonum est.               // "to fear is a good thing"
```

and it is reported that a comma was added (by who?), after 'timere':

```
Edwardum occidere nolite // in a single line, read:
timere, bonum est.       // "do not fear to execute Edward, it's good"
```

In any language there are reserved words, sacred or forbidden, and you must replace them: e.g. American "my gosh", instead of a forbidden word.

In any language there are pronouns, a grammatical form referring to another form, and whenever referencing, ambiguities may occur:

"because of the rain, Paul arrived late at the dentist. He was unhappy"

Who was unhappy? The dentist or Paul?

Ambiguity does not exist in computers, but *"errare humanum est"*. A human mistake can lead to misinterpretation. Keywords, punctuation and a misused pronoun are often error prone in JavaScript. This chapter is meant to guard you against such mistakes, and also meant to teach some programming best practices: design patterns.

7.1. Reserved words

The table below contains 38 words to which 10 more are reserved for future use:

debugger, enum, export, implements, import, interface, *package, private, protected, public*

Keyword	Use
`const, let, var, typeof`	Declarations. Type operator
`break, case, continue, default, do, else, false, for, if, switch, true, while`	Syntax of conditional instruction, branch or loop. The use of 'continue' is discouraged in loops, and the use of 'break' is encouraged in switch
`delete, in, instanceof, new, null, this` `class, extends, static, super`	Operators linked to objects Syntax of 'class' in ES6: ignored in this book.
`arguments, function, return, this, yield`	Syntax of function, or generator functions (yield)
`try, catch, finally, throw`	Exception handling
`eval, with`	Strongly discouraged use
`void`	Evaluates the expression to undefined
`yield`	Used with generator functions
`await`	Ignored in this book

Table 7.1. *Uses of reserved words*

These words are "reserved" and cannot be used for variables, functions and parameters, but can be property keys, though the dot notation is forbidden for them:

```
let const = 3;                    // illegal
const object = {const: 3};        // illegal
const object = {"const": 3};      // ok
const object["const"] = 4;        // ok
```

Besides reserved, it is wise to avoid using built-in objects names, methods or property names of the global object:

```
Object, Function, Array, Boolean, Number, String, Symbol, RegExp, Date,
Math, JSON, parseInt, parseFloat, isNaN, ...
```

Also, 16 words were "reserved" before ES5, and it is wise to avoid them as well:

```
abstract, boolean, byte, char, double, final, float, goto, int, long,
native, short, synchronized, throws, transient, volatile
```

7.2. The pronoun "this"

In object-oriented programming, any instruction is in the context of one object: the global object or a particular object. The role of the pronoun "this" is to tell which of these objects the instruction is dealing with, within its global/function scope. At the origin of JavaScript, the pronoun "this" has been introduced to determine which HTML DOM object is currently handled, and by default, it points to window, the HTML global object.

With the multiplication of the uses of JavaScript, this initial choice is a kind of "handicap". It is important to be trained on *this* in order to avoid mistakes.

7.2.1. *The many ways to link the pronoun "this"*

To keep it simple, we do not mention the *"use strict"* mode, where, roughly speaking, if this is not defined in some way, it is "undefined".

7.2.1.1. *First branch: global scope versus (local) function scope*

– In the global scope, this refers the global object,

```
// in the browser environment:
console.log(this === window); // true
// in Node.js, each module has its own global object:
console.log(this === global); // true
```

– In the function scope, the question to answer is: how is the function invoked?

7.2.1.2. *Function invoked with the operator (.)*

```
const f = function () {return this;};
f();                    // returns global by default [object Window]
```

7.2.1.3. *Function invoked as an object method*

```
const obj = {};
obj.myMethod = function () {return this;};
obj.myMethod();         // returns [object obj]
```

7.2.1.4. *Function invoked as a "callback" (DOM events, AJAX requests, etc.)*

```
const nav = document.querySelector('nav'); // <nav> tag
const toggNav = function (){ console.log(this);};
nav.addEventListener('click',toggNav);      // this = <nav> element
const xhr = new XMLHttpRequest();
xhr.addEventListener("load",jsonCallback); // this = "xhr" element
```

7.2.1.5. *Function coded in the "arrow syntax"*

Within an "arrow function", this retains the value of the enclosing lexical context this.

7.2.1.6. *Function invoked as "constructor" by the operator new*

See section 7.3: "Operator new".

7.2.1.7. *Multiple invocations: Inner function redefining "this"*

WARNING.– An inner function may change the value of this depending on the way that function has been invoked.

Here is a frequent issue: the inner function is a method of window object:

```
const nav = document.querySelector('.nav'); // <nav class="nav">
const toggNav = function () {
    console.log(this);       // <nav> element
    setTimeout(function () { // callback
        console.log(this);   // [object Window] !Beware!
                      }, 1000);
};
nav.addEventListener('click', toggNav, false);
```

One solution for passing the context value: copy this in that (usual name):

```
let that = this;
setTimeout(function () { console.log(that);   // <nav> ok!
                       }, 1000);
```

A simpler (ES6) solution is to use the arrow syntax:

```
setTimeout( () => { console.log(this);        // <nav> ok!
                  }, 1000);
```

7.2.2. How to explicitly bind the pronoun?

There are several approaches. We have seen two in the previous example: an intermediate variable (that) or the arrow syntax, but we cannot use these in every situation. Here are some more generic approaches.

"Binding mode"	Instructions	Result

No binding	`function sum(z) {`
	`    return this.x + this.y + z;`
	`}`
	`sum(3);`
		NaN

As an object property	`const context = {x: 1, y: 2};`
	`context.sum = sum;`
	`context.sum(3);`
		6

Using call	`sum.call( context, 3 );`	6
Using apply	`sum.apply( context, [3] );`	6
Prior binding using bind	`const s = sum.bind(context);` `s(3);`	6

Table 7.2. *Several ways to binding the pronoun in a function*

7.3. Operator: new

As already stated, we recommend to retrain the use of new but, in some cases, it must be used with built-in objects such as RegExp (Chapter 3), or XMLHttpRequest (Chapter 10). Therefore, we mention in this section, the impact of new on the binding of this.

Invoked with new, a function creates an object and modifies the value of this to the new object. In general, the returned value is precisely the value of that `this`, unless you specify an explicit different object (no reason to do so voluntarily). But this constructor function can be called as a regular function, using the operator (): then, we can also bind the function to give its `this` a different value. Remember the example in Chapter 4:

```
const c1 = new Candidate();    // object Candidate, no initialisation
Person.call(c1, last, first); // constructor Person initializes c1
```

7.4. Punctuation signs

Most punctuation signs play a role in JavaScript: some are polymorph, which means having different roles depending on the context.

Sign	Uses	P
" " ' ' ` `	Three kinds of quotes to delimit strings: double and simple (that you may mix if quotes are inside the string), and back-tick, for template string	
;	Ends an instruction, or empty instruction (if alone)	
,	List separator: object literal, array literal, or; Repetition operator in declaration instructions: let a, b, c;	P
.	Syntax to access an object property (dot notation)	
:	Syntax for ternary operator after ?, or; Syntax for key:value in object literal, or; Syntax for a switch case, or for a label just before a block {code}	P
?	Syntax of the ternary operator	
!	Unary boolean operator for negation. Used twice, it makes a boolean context: (for instance if x=4, !!x === true)	
!= !== == ===	Comparison operators: equality or inequality, make a boolean context	
> < >= <=	Relational operators. Implicit call to Object.prototype.valueOf() when comparing primitive values	
+	Binary arithmetic operator of addition, or the following String concatenation operator, or unary (see);	P
- * / % **	Binary arithmetic operators of subtraction, multiplication, division, rest (module) and exponentiation (left to right evaluation)	

+ -	Unary operators to convert into a positive/negative number, if impossible: yields NaN
++ --	Unary operators of incrementation, decrementation: can be used in prefix or postfix: ++x or x++
|| &&	Binary boolean operators of disjunction and conjunction: make a boolean context (left to right evaluation)
>> >>> << ^ | & ~	Binary bitwise operators: right-shift, unsigned right-shift, left-shift, Exclusive-or (XOR), logical or, and (OR/AND) Unary operator to invert bits
=	Assignment operator. Can be combined with: - an arithmetic operator, prefix: += -= *= /= **= %= - a bitwise operator, prefix: >>= >>>= <<= &= |= ^=
{ }	Syntax of object literal objet, or: Block of instruction for a function, a branch or a loop, or just plain: { let x; } creates a block **P**
[ ]	Syntax to access an object property, including an array element
( )	Grouping operator, with a list of parameters or arguments, or; Precedence operator: forces the immediate evaluation of the innermost pair of parentheses, or; Syntax for condition in branch or loop: if() for() while() **P**
...	Syntax (ES6) for objects or arrays: "rest syntax", "spread syntax"
=>	Syntax (ES6) for "arrow functions"
// /**/	Comments: end of line only Comments: possibly over several lines (warning: comments cannot be nested)

Table 7.3. *Punctuation signs used in JavaScript (col. P= polymorphism)*

7.5. JavaScript usual design patterns

In software development, a *"design pattern"* is a code pattern recognized as best practice to answer a certain conception issue and reusable for several situations.

We have already come across such patterns: to save free variables within a closure, to build a prototypal object with given prototype and properties, etc. By contrast, a pattern that is not easily reusable depending on a free context (global variables, etc.) is called an *"anti-pattern"*, even if it is working in its particular context.

The simpler forms of patterns are sometimes called "idioms", and more complex ones are categorized in the literature as:

– "creational patterns": the prototypal approach, in Chapter 4, is a creational pattern;

– "structural patterns": beyond creation, the "namespacing" and the "decorator" modules are structural patterns;

– "behavioral patterns": the "observer" and its "publish/subscribe" variant are behavioral patterns.

7.5.1. *Programming idioms*

7.5.1.1. *Default initializations using a logical shortcut*

Evaluating expressions in *boolean context*, e.g. conditional instructions, forces the variables to be cast as booleans instead of their own type. This leads to defining some default initialization idioms:

```
const localObjet = objet || {"nom":"default object"};
let localNum = num !== 0? (num || numDefaut) : 0;
let localStr = str !== ""? (str || strDefaut) : "";
let localProp = "prop" in objet? prop : propDefaut;
```

depending on the polymorphism of `false`, with respect to various values or types:

```
0, NaN, "", null, undefined → false (boolean)
```

7.5.1.2. *Encapsulation using a closure*

A frequent situation: we need an external control variable within the code block of a function, example:

```
let once = true;                // variable de contrôle externe
function printOnce(str){
      if (once) {once = false; return str;}
   // implicit else = return undefined
}
```

Solution: build a closure around both the variable and the code block, then return the inner code as a function expression:

```
function printOnce() {
  let once = true;
  return function(str){
      if (once) {once = false; return str;}
  };
}
const printOneTime = printOnce();
console.log(printOneTime("Hello"));    // -> Hello
console.log(printOneTime("Hello"));    // -> undefined
```

7.5.1.3. *Displaying the properties of an object: "Map/Entries Combo"*

Using the built-in object Map (ES6), an *"Iterable"* with a size property, and set and get methods, in combination with Object.entries:

```
const can = { nom: 'Good', prenom: 'Morning' };
const canMapped = new Map(Object.entries(can)); // idiom
canMapped.get('nom');    // -> 'Good'
canMapped.size;          // -> 2
```

Using Map in combination with Array from for a time series data array:

```
const timeData = [['d1', 'v1'], ['d2', 'v2']];
const timeMap = new Map(timeData);
timeMap.get('date1'); // returns "v1"
timeMap.forEach(function(v,d){console.log(`date ${d}, v= ${}`);});
const dates = Array.from(timeMap.keys())); // ["d1", "d2"]
const valus = Array.from(timeMap.values()));    // ["v1", "v2"]
```

7.5.2. *Creational pattern: "Assign/Create Combo"*

We have learned that we can combine one inheritance by delegation (shared) and several inheritances by concatenation (duplicated).

```
const obj = Object.assign(
      target [=Object.create(proto)], // provides the prototype
      source1,        // one source of properties
      source2         // anonther source
);
```

The object obj receives the properties of the sources and has proto as prototype. This pattern can be adapted to answer several needs.

7.5.2.1. *Read a JSON object and give it a prototype*

Data are often exchanged over the Internet in text files using JSON format, and this is an advantage for JavaScript: the assign/create combination can easily fit that use: Object.assign "mixes" a clone of the JSON parsed object, with a prototype independently provided by Object.create.

```
const base = {
  // JSON data
};
const proto = {
  // prototype methods
};
const nu = Object.assign(
  Object.create(proto),
  base)
);
```

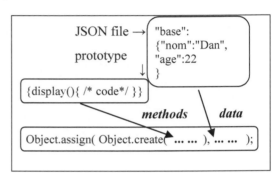

The object nu inherits by delegation of the methods of proto, while copying the properties of base. We have learnt that proto can be built from a function, thus providing a constructor.name:

```
function Nu(){}// "prototype support" + "constructor.name"
Nu.prototype.method1 = function(){/*...*/};
Nu.prototype.method2 = function(){/*...*/};
const proto = Nu.prototype;
const nu = Object.assign(Object.create(proto), base));
// nu is a "Nu" object (constructor.name === "Nu")
```

For an array of objects from the JSON file, and a given Nu.prototype, a single function call can build the entire nu's array, even choosing the properties to keep, or adding some. Let us wrap up everything here.

7.5.2.1.1. Complete pattern: "Assign/Create Combo"

```
function Nu(){}
Nu.prototype.email = function(){console.log("Dear "+this.nom);};
const dataset = [{"nom":"Dan"},{"nom":"Bob"}];  // JSON array
const nus = dataset.map(function(d,i){
  let nuPlus = {"n":(20+i)};    // if any is to be added
```

```
  delete d.uselessprop;                  // if any is not to be kept
  return Object.assign(Object.create(Nu.prototype), d, nuPlus);
});
```

checking it up:

```
nus.forEach( x=>{ x.email(); });          // "Dear Dan" / "Dear Bob"
console.log( nus[0].constructor.name);          // "Nu"
console.log( nus[0] instanceof Nu);             // true
console.log( Nu.prototype.isPrototypeOf(nus[0]));    // true
```

This pattern allows us to cumulate all the advantages:

– cloning the initial object (from JSON);

– customizing the clone by additions/deletions;

– inheriting by delegation from a given prototype;

– identification through a "constructor" name.

Though the operator nu instanceof Nu works here, it is safer to use the test Nu.prototype.isPrototypeOf(nu) (see Eric Elliott quote[1]: *"Don't listen to instanceof, and it will never lie to you"*).

7.5.3. *Structural pattern: singleton or namespace pattern*

The goal is to embed in a single object (singleton) all the data and tools relative to a certain apparatus, thus providing a unique global access: everything inside, which can be publicly visible, will be accessed through a single name. Therefore, it is called a *"namespace"*. For instance, a web page can be represented by a singleton: title, different sections, navigation tools, are all related: webpage.title, webpage.section[i], webpage.load(), etc.

If the initialization of the singleton requires external information (e.g. a JSON file), the pattern is not merely "creational"; it must be "structural" in that it combines the public data and methods, with a larger range of private variables and functions. The entire structure must be protected from the outside, and must have no side effect as well.

---

1 See medium.com/javascript-scene/why-composition-is-harder-with-classes-c3e627dcd0aa.

Let us develop this and tour its capabilities:

```
const webpage = (function() {   // first protection with const
    // defined within the local scope
    const privateM1 = function() { /* ... */ }
    const privateM2 = function() { /* ... */ }
    let privateP = 'foobar';
    const obj = {        // the "revealing pattern"
        publicMethod1: privateM1,
        properties:{publicProp: privateP}, // nested levels
        utils:{publicMethod2: privateM2}
    };
    Object.seal(obj);   // protection of structural changes, or
    Object.freeze(obj); // total protection against changes
    return obj;
})();
```

7.5.3.1. *Augmenting the previous namespace*

If it exists already, we use it as argument for the IIFE, otherwise we use an empty object. The "augmentation" is concentrated in a single instruction, the IIFE, which modifies the object window.webpage (or a copy, if webpage is frozen).

```
// webpage (the namespace name) can be modified locally and isn't
// overwritten outside of our function context
(function(webpage) {
    // new public methods and properties
    webpage.foobar = "foobar";
    webpage.sayHello = function() {alert("hello world");};
    // check whether 'webpage' exists in the global scope
    // if not, assign window.namespace an object literal
}) (window.webpage = window.webpage || {});
// if "frozen" or "sealed", first copy webpagePlus = webpage
```

7.5.4. *Another structural pattern: the Decorator pattern*

Somehow similar to augmentation, the "decorator" brings new methods to an object: wrapping them with the old ones into a new prototype. Hence, the decorator pattern is also called the "wrapper pattern".

Indeed, what the decorator does is to mix inheritance by delegation (the first prototype is the generic decorator) and inheritance by concatenation (the second prototype is the actual decorator, and you can build several).

7.5.4.1. *Code*

```
        // helpers: protoChainOf(), methodCalls()
function list(q,i){
   return `${protoChainOf(q, `= `, 0)}\n methods:
${methodCalls(q)}`;
}
function User(){return 'User only';}
function Age(){return 'Age only';}
function UserAge(){return "Mixin";}
User.prototype.full = function(){return this.first+"
"+this.last;};
Age.prototype.year = function(){return 2017 - this.age;};
let z1= Object.assign(Object.create(User.prototype),
Age.prototype),
    z2= Object.assign(Object.create(zu1),
{constructor:UserAge});
const last= 'Bel', first= 'Jo', age= 28, qqs= [];
qqs.push( Object.assign(Object.create(z1), {first,age}) );
qqs.push( Object.assign(Object.create(z2), {first},{age}) );
        // dynamic modification of methods
Age.prototype.year = function(){return 2018 - this.age;};
User.prototype.full = function(){return "M. "+this.last;};
console.log( qqs.reduce(function(s,q,i){return
s+list(q,i);},""));
```

7.5.4.2. *Logs*

```
User only, prototype chain=
 {last:Bel, first:Jo, age:28} (1)-> User [year] (2)-> User [full] (3)-> Object []
 methods: year:1989, full:M. Bel
Mixin, prototype chain=
 {last:Bel, first:Jo, age:28} (1)-> UserAge [] (2)-> User [year] (3)-> User [full] (4)       ->
Object []
 methods: year:1989, full:M. Bel
```

7.5.4.3. *Comments*

The prototype chain is correctly incremented and methods are delegated along. But, in case of subsequent changes, only those of User.prototype are passed on (see: the "M."), not those of Age.prototype: function year is a copy and not a reference to the method year of Age.prototype.

The "decoration" works, but this form of multiple inheritance remains static: there is no automatic update. The next pattern may be a solution to this issue.

7.5.5. Behavioral pattern: the observer or publish/subscribe pattern

This pattern is able to establish a one-way communication with modules that play the role of "*observers*". When notified, an *observer* reacts according to the signal received from the "*observable*". Each *observable* maintains its list of *observers*. This is the "push" approach, and it is called the "*subscriber/publisher*" pattern. In the "pull" approach, it is the *observer* that maintains a list of observables, and it has the role of asking every *observable* in order to know about any change.

7.5.5.1. Code: The "push" approach: the code is on the observable side

```
const Observable = function() { this.observers = []; }
Observable.prototype = {
  subscribe(callback) {          // adds to the list
    let yet = this.observers.some(c => c === callback);
    if(!yet) this.observers.push(callback);
  },
  unsubscribe(callback) {                // remove from the list
    let i = this.observers.indexOf(callback);
    if(i>-1) this.observers.splice(i, 1);
  },
  publish(str) {                // notifies the list
    this.observers.forEach(c => {c(this.title+" "+str);});
  }
};
const Observer = function(n) {        // closure: creating observers
  const name = n;
  return function(str){console.log(str+" for "+name);}
};
        // let's create a newsletter and 2 subscribers
const subscriber1 = Observer("Bob");
const subscriber2 = Observer("Nora");
const blog = Object.assign(Object.create(Observable.prototype),
              {"title":"myBlog","observers":[]});
blog.subscribe(subscriber1);    // register an observer
blog.subscribe(subscriber2);    // register an observer
```

```
blog.publish('Jan.2018 issue');          // notifies a change
      // logs: ---------------------
//> "myBlog Jan.2018 issue for Bob"
//> "myBlog Jan.2018 issue for Nora"
```

Each observable owns its list of observers and communication methods. The observers, in this example, are closures: just a name and a callback.

The handling of DOM events (chapter 8) uses this pattern and many animation modules as well.

7.6. Metaprogramming with ES6

7.6.1. *"Reflection" by "Symbols"*

A new API has been introduced in ES6, which compounds three objects: Symbol, Reflect and Proxy. Symbol is concerned with the *"Reflection within implementation"*: to modify the behavior of some generic methods of the objects owning that Symbol. Thus, a Symbol is mid-way between an object descriptive property and a comment of a code block.

There exist several predefined Symbol ; here we present two examples:

– Symbol.toStringTag: specifies the return value of Object#toString instead of the unexplicit [object Object]

```
const can = {   // example with an object literal
  get [Symbol.toStringTag] () { return 'Candidat'; }
}
Object.prototype.toString.call(can); // -> '[object Candidat]'
```

– Symbol.replace specifies the return value 'String#replace'.

7.6.2. *New tool for measuring code performance*

The object Performance has been introduced recently, providing direct access to the inner clock, plus some information about browsing.

The method window.performance.now provides the time, in milliseconds, which we can subtract between two successive calls and get a true duration (ms).

PART 2

Client-Side JavaScript

Introduction to Part 2

We are now dealing with objects that are not part of the Core JavaScript, but are provided by the environment of the web page, through its (Application Programming Interface [API]) programming interface. The tree structure of the HTML document, known as DOM (Document Object Model) is equipped with tools to handle the DOM elements and the associated events. The browser provides objects for handling the DOM, and other objects, for persistent storage (Cookies and Local Storage), for background tasks (Workers), for external requests via the HTTP protocol, the XmlHTTPRequest object, or the global function Fetch, which leads us also to present asynchronous processing.

We are at the interface between the "Core JS" embedded in the browser and the client-specific features: the APIs linked to HTML and to HTTP.

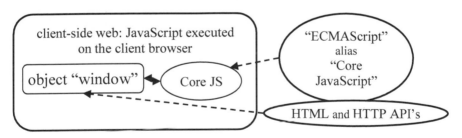

Core JavaScript objects and the objects of the environment

The ecosystem of the web page compounds three languages, HTML, CSS, JavaScript, and an HTTP protocol. Here is a short reminder, with comments on what may impact the JavaScript code:

– HTML dealing with the page content structure and semantics

A modern application adopts HTML5. What is fundamental to learn is the DOM. The following chapters will explain the tree structure and how to interact with it.

– CSS dealing with positioning and the cosmetics of DOM elements

A modern application adopts CSS2.1, plus some CSS3 modules (e.g. flex). What is fundamental to learn (from the JavaScript viewpoint) is the selection of the elements. A short chapter will recall these features.

– JavaScript dealing with dynamic modification and exchanges

A modern application adopts ES6. Assuming that the targeted applications are data oriented, it is useless to spend time on complying with older legacy systems. What is fundamental to learn are the notions of scope, prototype and functions as first-class objects. We will learn how this helps to correctly link the core parts and the various APIs of the window object. We will learn how to present data with graphics: plotting and animating.

– HTTP dealing with external requests that provide contents

A data-oriented application uses data repositories, served through specific APIs, and uses external scripts, provided by content delivery networks. What is fundamental to learn is how to make requests and how to manage responses. We will learn the technology AJAX and how to deal with JSON files in an asynchronous context.

The progress of standardization has been huge and all post-2015 browsers meet the standards recommended in this book.

JavaScript in the Web Page

8.1. Ecosystem of the web page: the HTML sequence

8.1.1. *Structure and semantics/layout and presentation*

HTML5 is said to be "semantical". What does it mean (in short)?

– When reading an activity report, we expect a title (also: author, date, etc.), an introduction, several sections, a conclusion, a table of contents, etc..

– When reading a newspaper, we expect a header (title, date), headlines and a few paragraphs, the usual rubriques: politics, world, culture, etc..

– On an e-commerce site, we expect product descriptions, society descriptions, online order tool, etc.

These expectations are quite usual and make sense: that is the *semantics*! The HTML5 semantic tags are meant to help search engines to figure out what is on a web page: <header>, <nav>, <main>, <sections>, <detail>, <figure>, etc.

Older tags are preserved, and new suggested practices may add to the semantics: e.g. a title tag should comply with its context, a <img> tag should contain a description (attribute alt="..."), etc.

8.1.2. *Reminder about HTML5 tags*

Here are the tags that, though not all mandatory, we recommend using to describing the context of your web page ecosystem.

```
<!DOCTYPE html>
<html lang="fr">
  <head>
    <title>Basic web page</title>
    <meta charset="utf-8">
    <link rel="stylesheet" href="style.css">
  </head>
  <body>
    <script id="code.js"> /* JavaScript code */ </script>
  </body>
</html>
```

8.1.2.1. *The DOCTYPE*

This informs the browser about what follows: in the above case, it is an HTML document (default HTML5). It could have been another kind of document, which needs a document type declaration (DTD) asking which engine to use, for example SVG:

```
<!DOCTYPE svg PUBLIC "-//W3C//DTD SVG 1.1 Tiny//EN"
      "http://www.w3.org/Graphics/SVG/1.1/DTD/svg11-tiny.dtd">
  <svg> <!- SVG code -> </svg>
```

After DOCTYPE, the <html> is generally split between <head> and <body>.

8.1.2.2. *The <head>*

The <head> contains:

– one <title> tag, mandatory in the standard: can be displayed by the browser;

– several <meta> tags:

```
<meta charset="utf-8"> is mandatory: gives the "charset" encoding
<meta name="viewport" ..> specifies the use of the viewport: recommended
```

– more possible <meta> tags (optional):

```
<meta name = " keywords " content = "...">
<meta name = " author " content = "...">
```

– one or several <link> tags for gathering CSS style sheets:

```
<link rel = "stylesheet" href = "./style.css" >
```

8.1.2.3. The <body>

The <body> may contain:

– a displayable content provided by "content tags", which are a pair of tags (opening–closing). For example, <div></div> creates a node 'div' plus a 'text' node, empty until it receives content (e.g. from JavaScript code);

– "empty tags", which create nodes containing instructions for the layout engine, such as the <br> tag (new line) or instructions to the HTTP daemon, asking for requests in parallel with the normal layout flow;

– the content of the corresponding nodes is not provided by the tag, but by some external asynchronous action[1]. For example, <img> tag: its attributes are meant to specify the request; the display[2] will come later if the request is successful (see the event loop in section 8.5).

– some comments <!- with this syntax ->,

Here is a list of the main empty tags:

```
<meta>, <link>, <base> within the <head>
<input>, <area>, in association with <map>
<source>, <track> in association with <picture>, <video>, <audio>
<img> instead, could be written: <picture><source></picture>
<hr>, <br>, <wbr> different line feeds
<colgroup> when the attribute span is present
```

Finally, <body> contains what matters to us the most: the <script> tag.

8.1.2.4. The <script> tag

In general, the script is in charge of filling in the tags inside <body>. It is wise to provide an initial content for those tags, making them quickly visible, even if they must be modified soon:

---

1 To find out how many requests a web page sends, use: webpagetest.org.

2 The closing sign (... />) is no longer required with empty tags. Writing into an empty tag with JavaScript has no effect.

```
<header>Web Data with JavaScript</header>
<main>curriculum 2018</main>
<footer>contact: IUT UPEM - Marne-la-Vallee</footer>
<script id="code.js">...code...</script>
```

Advantage: the page is never empty, the interpretation of the script may take a few seconds, and it "blocks" the next commands. Therefore, it is generally better to put the script tag at the end of <body>[3].

Suggestion: the id="code.js" attribute is a simple identification. If the code is in the text file "code.js", just replace id=par src="code.js".

DOCTYPE (mandatory) tells the browser that we use HTML5;   <html lang='..'> optional but useful attribute lang;   <meta charset='..'> tells which encoding is used (mandatory);   <meta viewport='..'> eases the viewport handling (*desktop vs. mobile*)   <title> mandatory in HTML5;   <link>(s) toward CSS stylesheets, or JSON files that you can "prefetch" using: <link rel="prefetch" href="/dataFile.json">   <body> with a few tags for quickly making visible minimal content.   <script id='..'> or <script src='..'>(s) -just before closing </body>

Table 8.1. *Overall recommendations for writing an HTML5 web page*

8.2. Building the web page DOM: the layout engine

The layout engine processes each content tag with the help of the relevant CSS rules (if any, see below) and displays content. Therefore, CSS rules must be at hand, preferably in the <head> part.

With empty tags, the layout engine can modify the normal flow (e.g.
 provokes a vertical offset), or prepare the expected result of an HTTP request (e.g. the alt attribute of <img> is displayed, and some room is provided for the picture to come). Such request are asynchronous, non-blocking.

NOTE.– Avoid plugins (Flash, Silverlight, Applets) that are doomed to disappear.

---

3 For highly intensive computational scripts, the "defer" and "async" attributes may help when using several script files (if there is a dependence order).

Once entirely browsed, the full set of tags will produce a tree structure, called the *Document Object Model* (DOM). The DOMContentLoaded event is triggered as soon as the DOM has been fully constructed.

The DOM is not part of JavaScript but an API allows JavaScript to interact with the DOM, which will be detailed in this chapter.

8.2.1. *DOM tree built by the layout engine: selecting nodes via CSS*

The HTML DOM is a tree: a root, followed by child nodes, recursively up to terminal nodes, empty-tags or text-nodes. The layout engine builds the tree while parsing the HTML document step by step in "depth-first" mode.

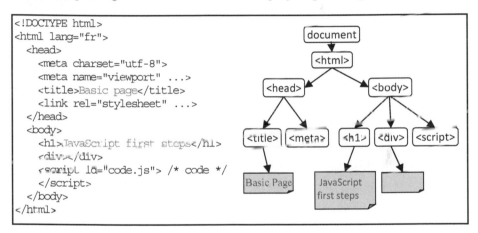

Figure 8.1. *HTML code (left) and associated DOM (right) built by the layout engine*

For each displayable node (gray in Figure 8.1), the layout engine uses a rendering rule: either from CSS or a browser-defined default value. That choice decision explores the different possibilities, from the most general to the most specific, hence the term cascade ("cascading style sheet").

8.2.2. *CSS rules and relationship with JavaScript selection methods*

The link between a DOM element and a CSS rule is established through the CSS selectors: a similar link can be established from JavaScript. JavaScript can also handle the CSS rules linked to a specific DOM element.

8.2.2.1. *CSS selector syntax*

```
selector {style_attribute: value, [style_attr: value, ...]}
```

selector = tag_name (div), or: .class_name (.menuItem), or: #identifier (#Bob18), plus optional modifiers:

- selector[attribute]   ex.: `input[focus]`

- selector:pseudo_class   ex.: `h1:hover, p:lang(fr), li:first-child`

- selector::pseudo-element   ex.: `p::first-letter, li::after{content:'..'}`

NOTE.– The CSS selector syntax is exactly the one used as argument with DOM API methods: `elt.querySelector(sel)` and `elt.querySelector All(sel)`.

8.2.2.2. *CSS cascade*

The uppermost and most recent rank wins:

- browser default: font, text color, block mode, margin, etc.;

- normal styles (and user < author), important styles (and author < user);

- and, if still the same rank, there is a disambiguation formula:

```
100*(#id) + 10*(.class, [attribut], :pseudo-class) + (tag, ::pseudo-elt)
```

Cosmetics rules (colors, fonts, borders, etc.) are easy to learn and handle. The positioning (relative, absolute) is much harder: it depends on both the element and the current state of the flow. It is suggested to learn the css-flexbox[4] module of CSS3 (horizontal and vertical positioning).

---

4 See http://the-echoplex.net/flexyboxes/.

8.3. Dynamic behavior of the web page: the script engine

When loading the page in the browser, several objects are created and stored in a tree structure called the "Browser Object Model" (BOM). In this structure, the window.document property refers to the DOM.

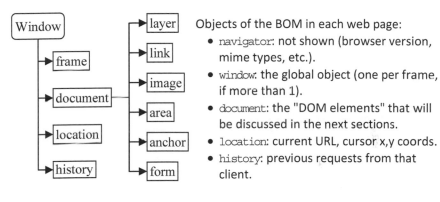

Objects of the BOM in each web page:
- navigator: not shown (browser version, mime types, etc.).
- window: the global object (one per frame, if more than 1).
- document: the "DOM elements" that will be discussed in the next sections.
- location: current URL, cursor x,y coords.
- history: previous requests from that client.

Figure 8.2. *Browser Object Model and Window object*

When the layout engine meets the tag <script>, it triggers the script engine, which loads (if external file) the code and starts its lexical analysis. That analysis is performed in the context of a global object = the object 'window' provided by the HTML API. It is a synchronous operation, which means that the HTML parsing is paused until the script engine has finished its job: it is worth placing <script> just before closing </body>.

Browser	Layout engine HTML + CSS	Script engine (JavaScript)
Firefox	Gecko	SpiderMonkey
Chrome	Blink	V8[5]
Internet Explorer	Trident	Chakra
Safari	WebKit	Nitro
Opera	Blink	V8

Table 8.2. *Layout engines and Script engines of major browsers*

When JavaScript starts, how does the communication with the DOM work?

---

5 V8: open-source project, written in C++ by Google for Chrome, used in Opera and Node.js.

– Context identification

The global object `window` gives access to many properties and methods, such as `window.document` and `window.alert` (to name a few). Also, all global variables and functions in the JavaScript code become embedded into the "window-namespace" and are explicit properties of `window`:

therefore:

are equivalent to:

```
const x = "un";              window.x = "un";
function f(){}               window.f = function(){};
```

The name of the global object can be omitted, hence we can remove the prefix `window` but we should always remember that it has an impact on the pronoun `this` (see section 7.2).

It is important to note that the object `window` is overcrowded with many properties from the browser, the DOM, AJAX objects, the built-in JavaScript objects, additional libraries... plus all our own global objects!

This is not only a code readability, traceability and reusability issue, this is also a performance issue. Indeed, everytime a variable is not local, it must be searched in the global object. Therefore, encapsulating the code within one function meant to wrap-up the entire application provides some performance gain. Such a function is named "the local function" and, for instance, it can be associated with the `window.onload` event or equivalent.

– Dialoging with the DOM

Be sure first that the document is ready: the object `window` can tell us via the event `load` or `domContentloaded`. Section 8.5 details that but, in short, let us use something simple (that event occurs just once, after all):

```
        /* before: any code that depends on nothing */
window.onload = function(){              // "handler"/"callback"
        /* here: code depending on the DOM. Only here we can be sure
            of the DOM being available for reading and writing */
};
        /* after: code not interacting with the DOM */
```

That process is *"asynchronous"*: the anonymous function is run when the load event is triggered: that function is called a *"handler"*, for it handles the event, and also a *"callback"* for the JavaScript code will be called back through that function (see Chapter 10).

Once the DOM is ready, the handler function interacts with the DOM via the object window.document and nested objects. Three functionalities are necessary to work with the DOM by:

– accessing individual DOM elements or a list of selected DOM elements with which to interact;

– reading and writing in those elements, creating new ones. We will detail two approaches (*lazy* and *constructive*);

– listening events and attaching them, specifically the callback functions to be triggered.

This chapter details these three aspects, their objects and methods.

8.4. Interface with the DOM

The root of the DOM tree is referred to by the property window.document or simply document. The nodes that we will handle are of the "element" type: document itself is the first one. We do not make use of the other types in this book ("text", "attribute", "comment"). In the following, several tables present a selection of the most useful methods and properties (there are so many of them in the API, many remaining as legacy). There are two basic objects: HTML DOM Element and its subobject HTML DOM Document.

Let us group these tools by functionality.

8.4.1. *DOM interface 1: selecting elements*

How to access node elements of the DOM? Since 2015 the answer is to use the methods querySelector and querySelectorAll.

EXAMPLES.–

```
const header = document.querySelector("header"); // tag <header>
const ihs = header.querySelectorAll("img"); // all <img> in header
```

The first line returns the first "HTML DOM Element" that is a <header>. The second line returns an "*array-like*", which lists all <img> elements in that header (if any). We will make intensive use of the method Array.from.

Thanks to the querySelector methods, we can recommend replacing:

– getElementsByTagName(tag), by querySelectorAll(tag);

– getElementsByClassName("clname"), by querySelectorAll(".clname");

– do not use the attribute id of a tag as a selector, its uniqueness is not guaranteed at all. Best practice: add the id value as a CSS class-name, which you may consider unique if you like, and select with querySelector:

therefore, replace:	with:

`<tag id="idv" class="cl">`
`...`
`el.getElementById("idval");`
	`<tag id="idv" class="idv clv">`
	`...`
	`el.querySelector(".idval");`

If idv is really unique, the right element will be correctly returned, otherwise we get only the first one, which is the same behavior as getElementById.

There are several advantages in using the querySelector methods:

– the CSS selectors syntax provides the same range of possibilities as the CSS itself. For example, elt.querySelectorAll("div [lang=de]");

– the CSS selectors must be learned anyway (two birds with one stone!);

– optionally, you can remove the risky use of the so-called unique identifier id="idv" and replace it with a more robust approach.

8.4.2. *DOM interface 2: reading/writing/creating an element*

8.4.2.1. *Reading or writing simple content (data)*

The selected element, corresponding to a content tag, has two properties, available for both operations:

– elt.innerHTML: all the HTML between <tag> and </tag>;

– elt.textContent: the content of the inner text-node within the element; useful for simple values, not formatted (a number, a string).

8.4.2.2. *Reading and writing attributes*

Use the methods elt.getAttribute or elt.setAttribute: they work for content tags and empty tags as well (ex. <img src=".." ..>).

8.4.2.3. *Creating new elements: the "lazy" method*

The target element is a content tag and we can consider a first approach, called "lazy", which is easy to code and useful for rapid prototyping.

It can be used when HTML code is simple or comes from an external source (e.g. an HTML fragment) which we do not need to parse first. Simply write that code: the layout engine automatically interprets the tags and infers the creation of nested elements into the target. For example:

```
let selec = ".slogan";        // CSS selector for class="slogan"
const devise = "JavaScript for everybody";
document.querySelector(selec).innerHTML =
        `maxim of the day: <b>${devise}</b>`;
const text = getTextFromSomeWhere( );     // HTML code block
document.querySelector("aside").innerHTML = text;
```

8.4.2.4. *Creating new elements: the "constructive" method*

This second approach is more complete and more robust. There are four steps:

– b1. create the new element: document.createElement("tag");

– b2. set content, and attributes;

– b3. attach handlers to events;

– b4. add this new element to the target, selected in the document.

Let us detail these steps as an example:

```
let nuElt = document.createElement("div");        // b1.
nuElt.setAttribute("class", "maxim");
nuElt.innerHTML = "maxim of the day";             // b2.
```

```
function handlerIdee(e){ alert("eureka" + e.target.innerHTML }
nuElt.addEventListener("mouseOver", handlerIdee);          // b3.
document.querySelector("article").appendChild(nuElt);      // b4.
```

There are three advantages to this approach:

– the three steps can be used separately: for instance, (b2) can be used recursively for nesting a list of second level tags;

– we can attach handlers before adding the element into the existing target;

– it has no impact on the DOM until step (b4), for example:

```
const helt = document.createElement("header");
helt.setAttribute("class", ...);
helt.addEventListener(event, function (){ ... });
...
window.onload = function(){
    document.querySelector(selector).appendChild(helt);
    ...
```

We will see that the order is important for the events: if the event is triggered before the handler is set, it will simply be ignored (too late).

8.4.3. *Methods for HTML DOM document and element prototypes*

The following tables list a selection of useful properties and methods, for data-oriented purposes, grouped by functionality.

There exist many more methods, dealing with navigating the DOM (nextChild, nextSibling, etc.) or handling text (direction, focus, scrolling, etc.). The reader may easily find the documentation on the Internet.

Selection of properties for HTML DOM Element

Properties	Description
elt.innerHTML, textContent	Returns or redefines the content of elt, or its text-node
elt.id, .title	Returns or redefines the attributes 'id' or 'title' of elt
elt.nodeName, nodeType, nodeValue	Returns name, type, value of a node
elt.offsetHeight, offsetWidth...	Returns height, width ... (including border ...) of elt
elt.parentElement	Returns the parent node of elt
elt.classList	Returns the class name(s) of elt
elt.style	Sets or returns the value of the style attributes of elt

Selection of methods for HTML DOM Element

Methods	Description
elt.addEventListener(), .removeEventListener()	Adds an event handler to the element Removes a specific handler
elt.appendChild(), .insertBefore(), .removeChild()	Adds a child node to elt, as a 'last child node', or just before a given child node or removes a node
elt.click()	Simulates a mouse-click on an element
elt.querySelector(), .querySelectorAll()	Returns the first, or the full collection of, inner nodes, according to the given CSS selector
elt.getElementsByClassName(), .getElementsByTagName()	Returns the collection of inner nodes complying with the class name or tag name (see recommendations)
elt.getAttribute(), .setAttribute(), .removeAttribute()	Returns the value of a specific attribute of the element, redefines and return an attribute value, or removes it

Selection of properties and methods for HTML DOM Document

Properties/methods	Description
document.getElementById()	Finds an element by element id (cf. note)
document.createElement()	Creates a HTML element
document.createElementNS()	Creates a HTML element in a specific namespace
document.head	Returns the <head> element
document.images	Returns all <img> elements

8.5. The events in client side JavaScript

There are several kinds of *events* in the ecosystem of the web page: the events triggered from a DOM element, from the document, or from window itself; the events triggered by objects interacting with the web page (e.g. loading an image, a video), or by objects created for an HTTP request: XMLHttpRequest.

8.5.1. *The browser event loop*

Each browser window runs only one process: the "*event loop*", which successively, and sequentially, executes the tasks.

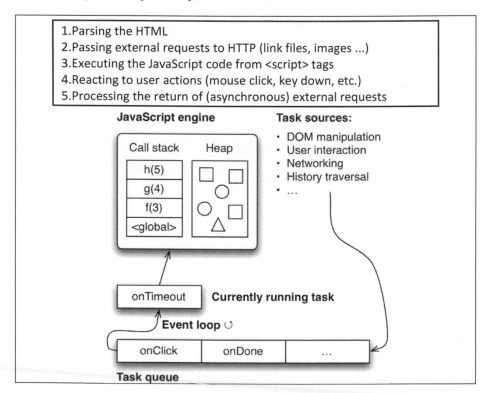

Figure 8.3. *The Browser event loop*[6]

6 Diagram excerpted from Philip Roberts: https://vimeo.com/96425312.

Several processes may run concurrently and can insert new tasks into that loop: window.requestAnimationFrame, window.setTimeOut, etc.

8.5.2. *Handling DOM events*

The DOM event handling is done in the following way:

– each DOM or BOM element (window) can support several events: "click", "error", "load", "input", "mouseover", ... depending on its type;

– an event is wrapped in an object owning general properties (see below), plus specific properties, such as the pixel coordinates of a "click";

– an event must have a *"handler"* attached to at least one complying element, in order to have an effect;

– an event can be propagated (e.g. to a parent node);

– JavaScript can attach one or several handlers to each element.

An event handler is a function meant to be called back after the event has been triggered: that function is called a *"callback"*, for its execution waits until the event occurs (or never). An object e representing the event is passed to that function. That object owns the following properties:

– e.type provides the name of the event: "click", "load", "error", etc.;

– e.timeStamp provides the creation time of the event (milliseconds);

– e.target is useful for distinguishing between elements if the same handler has been attached to all of them. Sometimes we may have to distinguish the element on which the event occurs (e.target) and the element to which the event is attached (e.currentTarget), depending on the propagation mechanism[7]: "capturing" or "bubbling".

Here is an example.

```
function theHandler(e){ // code run when the event is captured
   const elt = e.target;        // elt: has captured the event
}
const elt = [[element]];        // any DOM element supporting "click"
const hnd = elt.addEventListener("click", theHandler, false);
```

---

7 https://developer.mozilla.org/en-US/docs/Web/API/Event/currentTarget.

Let us explain that example:

– The *handler* is asynchronously listening to an event. The instruction `hnd = elt.addEventListener(type, handler [,capture])` tells the element `elt` to run the `handler` whenever an event `type` is captured: `addEventListener` attaches the handler to the [elt-type] couple.

– The *listener* returned by that method is stored in a variable `hnd`, which can be removed later using `removeEventListener(hnd)`. The optional parameter `capture` defaults to `false`, meaning that only the handler of the innermost element is activated; if `true` any handler of a parent element would be activated as well ("bubbling").

RECOMMENDATION.– The best practice is to use `addEventListener`.

There are two reasons for that recommendation:

– you can attach several *handlers* to an element-event pair, without overwriting[8] then, to identify and remove them individually.

– the event handling syntax is homogeneous for DOM events and other events[9], and more compliant with Core JavaScript rather than the DOM API.

This is one advantage of the constructive approach of creating DOM elements, adding event handlers at creation time, even before the DOM document is ready (only the last step, `appendChild` requires that). In cases where several resources are requested, concurrently with a request on DOM readiness, it is important to assign the *handlers* to the elements before appending them to the DOM. A typical example is requesting access to a video, and to the DOM, at the same time as adding that video:

– the *handler* for the video (listening to a video-loaded event) must be added to the video element before adding the video element to the DOM, because loading the video may be faster than executing the JavaScript code that adds a listener to an already created element of the DOM, in which case the video-loaded event is just lost (listened to too late).

---

8 If using `elt.onclick = handler;` you have a unique handler (subject to overwriting).

9 Handling events is not Client-side specific, it exists in Node.js, for instance: *https://nodejs.org/docs/latest-v5.x/api/http.html#http_event_connect*.

You never know which event will terminate first: the constructive approach is the only solution.

8.6. Interacting with the DOM: to link elements/events

8.6.1. *Waiting for the DOM*

Let us compare two "DOM ready", approaches:

```
function domReadyHandler(e){/* some DOM depending code */}
const start = window.addEventListener("DOMContentLoaded",
                                        domReadyHandler);        // 1
```

and

```
window.onDOMContentLoaded = domReadyHandler;                    // 2
```

The handler domReadyHandler contains all the querySelector calls and subsequent DOM interactions which actually modify the page content. The DOM instructions, such as creating and setting new elements, should rather be performed earlier: the constructive approach is therefore recommended.

Approach 1 is the best practice, however, the "old-style" alternative, approach 2, may be tolerated, for the event is handled just once and removing, or overwriting, has no effect.

The window object supports both load and DOMContentLoaded events. The later happens as soon as the HTML document has been loaded, not waiting for images, etc. The event load happens when the web page is totally loaded. You can choose which event fits your needs the best[10] (e.g. need for images or SVG).

8.6.2. *Example: to build an HTML list*

To build a menu, or a data list, we must fill in a <li> node, or a <table> node with inner <tr> and <td>, which has become a much easier operation since ES6.

---

10 [MIH 17].

– Lazy approach:

```
function htmUlList(){     // no parameter (accepts any number)
   function makeLi(acc, x){ return acc + `<li>${x}</li>`; }
   return Array.from(arguments).reduce( makeLi, "<u>") + "</u>";
}
document.querySelector("nav").innerHTML = htmULList("A", "B", "C");
// <ul><li>A</li><li>B</li><li>C</li></ul>
```

An undetermined number of arguments is passed to htmULList, then read from the arguments array-like variable, and turned into an array and processed by reduce. Then, the result is written into a <nav> element.

– Constructive approach (one handler per list item):

```
function clickList(e){alert(e.type+" "+e.target.textContent);}
function htmULList(){
   function makeLi(x){
      const el = document.createElement("li");
      el.textContent = x;
      el.addEventListener("click",clickList);
      return div.appendChild(el);
   }
   const div = document.createElement("ul");
   Array.from(arguments).forEach(makeLi);
   return div;   // div has been filled in with <li>s
}
document.querySelector("nav")
   .appendChild( htmULList("A","B","C") );
```

With the constructive approach, each <li> element can individually receive a handler. In that example, a click on "B" will alert "click B".

EXERCISE.– Use a closure and mutualize the code to implement htmULList and htmOList <ol>.

8.6.3. *Using events: modifying attributes and class names of an element*

8.6.3.1. *Stamping an element via one attribute (JavaScript to HTML)*

One handler can set an attribute for "stamping" an element once the event has been triggered: that element stores that "stamp", which can be checked later, using a selector tag[attribute=value]. This is an easy way to store

information into the HTML. Actually, the attributes `name` and `value` of
`<button>` are used that way, and we can also use `title` and even a custom
name (not "id", "href", "src" or alike). For example:

```
// to stamp paragraphs, then retrieve them
function stampParagraph(e){
    e.target.setAttribute("ok",true); // stamps <p> when clicked
}
document.querySelectorAll("p").forEach(function(x){
    x.addEventListener( "click", stampParagraph );
});
// ... somewhere:
document.querySelectorAll("p").forEach(function(x){
  if(x.getAttribute("ok")) console.log(x.textContent+" stamped");
});
```

8.6.3.2. *Dynamic handling of CSS styles*

Modifying the style, position or size of DOM elements, as a response to
some events, is an important task for animating data, visualizing the result of
a variety of computations, etc.

We can modify each individual feature upon request: for instance the
instruction `elt.style.display="none";` will just hide the element
from the layout engine refresh. But for more complex operations, it can be
preferable to prepare several CSS rules and then just choose the right rule at
the right time. It can be done with the object `ClassList` and its methods
that create, replace, or toggle individual classes in that list.

8.6.4. *Dispatching events, creating a CustomEvent*

There is a method allowing the code to trigger an event from an element,
for instance, emulating a "click" on a button:

```
const elo = document.querySelector("button");
elo.addEventListener('click', eventHandler); // listen for "click"
elo.dispatchEvent(new Event("click"));  // -> eventHandler();
```

We can define our own events with customized information:

```
const elt = document.createElement("div");      // event emiter
const evt = new CustomEvent('build', { detail: new Date() });
                    // event.detail: to pass additional data
```

```
elt.addEventListener('build',eventHandler); // listen for event
elt.dispatchEvent(evt);          // Dispatch the event
function eventHandler(e) {
    console.log( e.detail );     // Thu Oct 19 2017 17:58:00
}
```

We can use such events to activating a "Worker" (see Chapter 10).

9

Graphic and Multimedia Tools

The processing of data also requires graphic tools for visualization:

– to draw directly into the web page, from data array (vector format);

– to display pictures, from image or video sources (pixel format).

This chapter presents the HTML5 tools that JavaScript can use either for direct drawing (SVG or canvas) or multimedia display (images and videos). Displaying external sources requires sending an asynchronous request, whose return is handled, as seen in Chapter 8, by callbacks.

9.1. To draw in the web page

First, we need a surface onto which to place the drawing. There are three approaches, corresponding to the three following elements:

– <iframe>: this opens a new window, placed in a rectangle of the target window, although it is actually a different window from a different HTTP request and with an independent window object, and is hence a different window.document, an independent JavaScript engine with its own global space, etc. This is the oldest way to proceed, before the AJAX technology. We ignore it in this book.

– <svg>: SVG is a markup language, like HTML, and can be run with a specific layout engine. We can display an <svg> page, just as we display an <html> page. Moreover, SVG shares several features with HTML: (a) a document model similar to the DOM, and which can be "embedded" as a branch of the DOM so that the HTML layout engine is capable handling it;

(b) style rules in a CSS format, which can be included in the same style sheet. In Part 3, we present one cartographic application using <svg>.

– <canvas>: this is just a regular HTML5 element, like a <div>, attached to which is a "graphic context", an object with specific graphic methods.

9.1.1. *The elements <figure> and <canvas>*

Among the HTML5 *semantic tags*, the <figure> tag is meant for wrapping up graphic features, such as <img>, <video> or <canvas>, with a <figcaption> tag for its title or legend. We suggest using:

```
<figure>
 <img> ... or <video>, or <canvas>, ...
 <figcaption>Legend of the graphic element</figcaption>
</figure>
```

The element <canvas> provides a rectangular surface on the web page, which can be associated with a "graphic context", and JavaScript can have access to the properties and methods of that graphic context. For compatibility reasons, it is preferable to give an initial size (width, height) to the canvas element as well as some default text, which will be overwritten if everything works fine later with the JavaScript code.

Here is a simple example:

```
<canvas class="graf1" width="480" height="320">"graf 1"</canvas>
<script>
const canvas = document.querySelector('.graf1');
const ctx = canvas.getContext('2d');
ctx.fillRect(x,y, w,h);        // one method of canvas API
```

9.1.2. *2D curve plot*

9.1.2.1. *Drawing directly with the canvas methods*

This code shows how to plot an array coo[] as the graph of: y=coo(x).

```
function drawCurve(ctx, coo, lColor, lWidth, axix) {
  let min = coo.reduce(function(a, x) {return Math.min(a, x)});
  let max = coo.reduce(function(a, x) {return Math.max(a, x)});
  const offsetX = 20, offsetY = 20; // offset= room for X,Y-axis
  let basX = offsetX, basY = ctx.canvas.height - offsetY;
```

```
if (min < 0) {
     basY /= 2; max = Math.max(Math.abs(min), Math.abs(max))
  }
const incX = (ctx.canvas.width - basX) / coo.length,
      incY = basY / max;
ctx.save();                      // line 11: start drawing
ctx.beginPath();
ctx.strokeStyle = lColor; ctx.lineWidth = lWidth;
ctx.moveTo(basX, basY - coo[0] * incY);
coo.forEach(function(y, x) {      // y: value, x: index
  ctx.lineTo(basX + x * incX, basY - y * incY); ctx.stroke()
});
ctx.closePath();
ctx.restore();                      // line 19: end drawing
if(coox){ drawAxis(ctx.canvas, axix);}
}
```

The first 10 lines are preparing the necessary parameters for transforming the coo[] values into values in the coordinates space of the canvas (viewport transformation): basX, basY, incX, incY. The function drawAxis is not detailed: it is not necessary for our purpose and plotting the main curve is enough. Lines 11 to 19 develop that plot: methods save and restore preserve the current context; beginPath and closePath tell the plot to be a closed "path" (polygon); and forEach, which avoids using a loop, achieves that plot by calling lineTo and stroke. The path is plotted as a line (stroke, with strokeStyle); it could have been drawn as a surface (fill).

It is worth knowing the <canvas> mechanism and how to interact from JavaScript: this is why the function drawCurve has been detailed above. In practice, there is a range of solutions from light libraries to complete frameworks.

9.1.2.2. *Drawing with the Dygraph library*

The open source library Dygraph[1] is available under "MIT license". The object "Dygraph" accepts data tables from CSV or JSON files or directly from an array, and we can then plot that data into a <canvas>, with options for formatting the axis, etc.

---

1 See http://dygraphs.com/2.0.0/dygraph.min.js (121 kb).

Here, the code initializes the arguments to pass to the Dygraph object: the dataTable format must be: `[[number,number],..]` or `[[date,number],..]`.

```
let dataTable = insee.dataset.data;
let d00 = dataTable[0][0];           // check its type
let dygData = dataTable.reverse();   // ascending time
if( typeof d00 === "string" ) // string -> date
    dygData = dataTable.map(x=>{x[0] = new Date(x[0]); return x;});
let title = insee.dataset.name || "default title",
    width = 480, height = 200,
    axes = {
        x:{pixelsPerLabel: 30},
        y:{axisLabelFormatter(y) {return (y/1e6).toFixed(0)+"m";}}
    };
const g = new Dygraph(
    document.querySelector(".plot"),    // where to plot
    dygrafTable,                 // data (or url to a CSV file
    {title, width, height, axes}
);
```

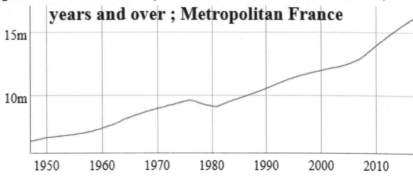

Figure 9.1. *Plotting chronological data using the Dygraph library*

A full example is provided in Part 3.

9.1.2.3. *Google Charts*

This is not a library, but a mostly outsourced environment[2]. It provides one object, "Data Table", into which we input the given 2D data array, somewhat similar to the Dygraph's library, and then data are translated into a two-level HTML5/SVG mix. The first level is a dynamic loader, which we can download (108 k), and the second level runs in the Google Cloud and can be chosen among different modules (Bar, Bubble, Histogram, etc.). Therefore you are stuck in the Google realm (no local version). An application, using the Gantt module, is presented in Part 3.

9.1.2.4. *D3.js*

This is an open source library, under "BSD 3-clause". A framework for "Data-Driven Documents" (D3), it uses a range of web tools, as their motto says: "D3 brings data to life using HTML, SVG, and CSS".

9.1.2.5. *Note about 3D graphics*

Since 2017, most browsers support the WebGL API for 3D graphics[3] on the web. This technology gives access to the OpenGL ES (Open Graphics Library for Embedded Systems) standard.

9.2. SVG language

"Scalable Vector Graphics" (SVG) is a markup language, like HTML, compatible with browsers supporting XHTML, such as HTML5. It allows the user to design graphic elements (curves, surfaces) and handle them as vector data. It results from a working group formed in 1998 by IBM, Apple, Microsoft, Xerox, etc.

A web page can be stand alone SVG, starting with (or similar to):

```
<!DOCTYPE svg PUBLIC "-//W3C//DTD SVG 1.1//EN"
                      "http://www.w3.org/Graphics/SVG/1.1/DTD/svg11.dtd">
<svg>  here: the SVG code      </svg>
```

---

2 See https://developers.google.com/chart/interactive/docs/.
3 Documentation and examples: https://threejs.org.

Alternatively, it can be a HTML document embedding the same SVG code, with the SVG style rules possibly moved into the <style> element. Here is an example:

```
<style>
  svg {position:absolute; left:10px; top:10px; width:480px; height:340px}
  .p0 {stroke:black; stroke-width:0.1; fill:white}
  .r0 {fill:blue} .euro {fill:yellow} .memberstate {fill:green}
</style>
<body>
  <svg xmlns="http://www.w3.org/2000/svg" viewBox="0 0 230 192.5">
  <g class="maing" transform="translate(-9,-9)">
   <rect class="r0" x="10" y="10.1486" width="228.023" height="189.851">
   <g class="pays memberstate" id="Monaco">
     <path class="p0" d="M83.6619 151.193c-0.2476,0.0627 -0.5932,0.1566 -
0.9258,0.2615l0 0 0.0691 -0.4229c0.2099,-0.203 0.4828,-0.1426 0.7337,-0.1075
0.0318,0.0044 0.0933,0.259 0.123,0.2689l0 0z" />
   </g>
  </g>
  <!-- <g> more countries </g> -->
  </svg>
</body>
```

The layout engine, when analyzing the <svg> element, is informed of which type of SVG is to be processed (xmlns attribute). Then the engine can translate the <svg> inner elements and add them to its own DOM.

Those elements can be accessed by both CSS and JavaScript (same selectors), with additions: for example, stroke or fill attribute in CSS, and a bunch of methods of the object "SVG Element", for instance r.isPointInFill(pt) determines if the point pt is inside the r polygon.

Available tags are <rect>, <circle>, <ellipse>, <polygon>, <text>, <marker>, etc. and also <path>, described below, and <g> which allows the user to group several tags together and possibly apply the same operation to all of them: a CSS style or a geometric transformation.

The tag <path> represents a set of elementary simple plots between two positions: line segments, circle arcs, quadratic or Bézier curve fragments.

This example is the border line of Monaco (a rather short <path>), and it is the succession of three Bézier fragments (with bold letters for ease of reading):

```
<path d="M83.66 151.2c-0.247,0.063 -0.59,0.16 -0.93,0.26 0 0.069 -
0.423c0.21,-0.203 0.483,-0.142 0.734,-0.1075 0.032,0.0044 0.0933,0.259
0.123,0.269 0z">
```

The first, 'M' (moveTo), sets the start position of the plot, then the letter 'c' (curveTo) plots a curve from that position, using three or more control points to define the Bézier, and then again up to the letter 'z' which signals for the path to be closed, back to the start position.

This example is an excerpt from the SVG file used in Part 3 (countries of Europe): the initial rectangle is filled in blue (oceanic background), and then the countries are filled in white with a black contour (their borders).

There is a specific framework to handle SVG in JavaScript: SNAP. Snap.svg is an open-source library, available under an Apache 2 license. It provides several features that make animations easier in SVG.

9.3. Handling time in graphics animation

9.3.1. Methods setTimeout, setInterval, requestAnimationFrame

Handling the real time elapsed is useful when waiting for an answer (not too long) or monitoring an evolution (not too fast). The window object proposes two methods which allow the execution of a function at a specific time or by specific intervals:

– window.setTimeout(*func*, *x*) runs func, after a given x milliseconds;

– window.setInterval(*func*, *x*) repeats running func every x milliseconds.

Both methods return an object reqId, whose effect can be canceled, respectively, by window.clearTimeout(reqId) or clear Interval(reqId).

For graphic data animation, the following method of the object window should be preferred:

```
-window.requestAnimationFrame(callback, x)
```

Instead of relying on time (approximately good), this method requests the next available frame in the queue of the graphic scheduler. The callback function updates the data, then generally asks again for the next frame, which will refresh the drawing onscreen. The returned value (*reqId*) can be used somewhere else by the cancelAnimationFrame(*reqId*), if cancelling the refresh is necessary. For example:

```
<p style="width:0; height:0; background-color:red"></p>
<script>
let start = null, mover = null;
let maxDuration = 2000; // equiv. 120px if 1px/frame = 60 frames/s
function step(timestamp) {
  function update(elt) {
    let wdth = parseInt(elt.style.width);
    elt.innerHTML = "<b>"+(100*wdth/6).toFixed(0)+"</b>";
    elt.style.width = elt.style.height = (wdth+1)+'px';
    return (timestamp - start); // approx. 100*wdth/6 (1/60s)
  }
  if (!mover)
      {start = timestamp; mover = document.querySelector('p');}
  /* updates the content of a given element */
  if (update(mover) < maxDuration) {requestAnimationFrame(step);}
}
window.onload = function(){requestAnimationFrame(step);};
```

The example gives rise to a rectangle (a <p> element) from 0 to 120px.

NOTE.– How do we transform speed from pixel-per-frame to pixel-per-second?

$$1 \text{ pixel/frame} = 1 \text{ pixel/60 s} = 60 \text{ pixel/s}$$

If we need to move at n pixel/s, the increment must be (n/60) pixels at each frame. In the example, an increment = '1px' makes the square grow by '120px' in 2 s (2,000 ms).

We cannot see an animation in this book, but here is a simple code for drawing a complex fractal plot: http://slicker.me/fractals/animate.htm.

9.3.2. *Performance considerations, generator functions*

9.3.2.1. *Improve thing performance of an animation on <canvas>*

Before animating a graphic application, we should separate parts that have to be animated from those which remain fixed. We should then prepare a <canvas>, or a simple <div> meant to receive the fixed parts, and then place, above that element, the <canvas> that is to be animated, with its background set to transparent. We may even split our set of animated objects between those which are permanently updated and those that change only on occasion. It is preferable to not scale the canvas, but if we have to, it is better to start with a smaller canvas and scale up, rather than start with a bigger canvas and scale down.

9.3.2.2. *Using "generator functions" in an animation*

A new ES6 tool, a "generator function", whose syntax is function*, allows us to simulate a series of functions whose successive calls only run some fragments, delimited by as many yield operators as we need in order to simulate that series of "functions". For example:

```
const acts = ["motion","beam","backbeam1","beam","backbeam2"];
function* animGenerator(arr) {
  const act = ()=>console.log(`anim. ${arr.shift()}`);
  let x = arr.length, y, z, t;
  act(); y = 2 * (yield (x + 1));
  act(); z = yield (x + y/3);
  act(); t = yield (x+y+z);
  act(); return (t + 1);
}
const gen = animGenerator(acts);
let nextanim, delay;
do{
  nextanim = gen.next(delay);        // first delay=null
  delay = nextanim.value;
  console.log( "delay= "+ delay +", actions left: "+ acts.length);
}while(!nextanim.done)
console.log( "animGenerator is done");
```

EXPLANATION.–

The generator function is able to produce four different outputs; it contains three yield instructions and one return. Its inner function act consumes one element of the array given as argument, and logs every next call onto the console.

The generated function gen stores the array argument's size in variable x, which will be used several times. For each gen.next, the yield(exp) terminates a fragment of code and returns the object {done:false, value:[[exp]]}. The return returns {done:false, value:[[exp]]}:

Call	Operation	Result
next#1	x= 5 (initial closure), y = 2*(5+1),	x + 1 = 6
next#2	x=5, y=12,	x+ y/3 = 9
next#3	x=5, y=12, z=9,	x + y + z = 26
return	x=5, y=12, z=9, t=26	{done:true, value:27}.

Table 9.1. *Behavior of a generator function (example)*

NOTE.– In the case where there is no return instruction, the next next returns {done:true}. More calls would have no effect and it always returns {done:true}.

We use that mechanism for generating a series of simulated animations starting or ending: it is more explicit than checking everytime among a set of possible choices. Here is the output of our example:

Inside each gen.next()	After
"anim: motion" "anim: beam" "anim: backbeam1" "anim: beam"	"delay= 6, actions left: 4" "delay= 9, actions left: 3" "delay= 26, actions left: 2" "delay= 27, actions left: 1" "animGenerator is done"

Table 9.2. *Results of a sequence of next calls to the generator function*

9.4. Data persistence between client sessions

9.4.1. *Http cookies*

The mechanism of the "Http cookie" was introduced by Netscape in 1995, the same year as JavaScript. It allows the user to link a server in order to store a few data related to successive requests of a same client. Each "cookie" is a small information block, in the format *"name=value;expires=expDate;"*, with a maximum size of 4 kb and stored in a file of 300 cookies maximum.

We can access that file with `window.document.cookie`.

Here is an example of using a "cookie", excerpted from the *w3schools* tutorial.

```
function setCookie(cname,cval,exdays) {
  const d = new Date();
  d.setTime(d.getTime() + (exdays*24*60*60*1000));
  const expires = "expires=" + d.toGMTString();
  document.cookie = cname + "=" + cval + ";" + expires +
";path=/";
}
function getCookie(cname) {           // returns "username"
  const na = cname + "=",
        va = decodeURIComponent(document.cookie).split(na);
  return (va[1].split(";"))[0] || "";
}
function checkCookie() {
  let user = getCookie("username");
  if (user !== "") { alert("Welcome again " + user);}
  else {
    user = prompt("Please enter your name:","");
    if (user) { setCookie("username", user, 30);}
  }
}
```

Though not a sophisticated technology, it is still in use, billions of times every day. Today's "drill, baby, drill" becomes: "track, baby, track".

9.4.2. *Local storages*

In order to improve that persistence even more, HTML5 introduced the `window.localStorage` object, whose API gives access to a 'sessionStorage' or a permanent 'localStorage'. These objects, attached to a domain name, allow us to store and update a much larger set of data than cookies.

EXAMPLE.– Counting 'clicks' on a button. Put this code in the handler:

```
if(typeof Storage !== "undefined") { //object Storage is supported
    if (localStorage.clickcount) {
       localStorage.clickcount = Number(localStorage.clickcount)+1;
    } else {localStorage.clickcount = 1;}
    // console.log( localStorage.clickcount + " time(s)." );
}
```

Object	Purpose
window.localStorage	For saving key/value pairs in a browser : no expiration date
window.sessionStorage	For saving key/value pairs in a browser : one session only
Property / Method	Description
length	Number of 'data items' stored in the storage object
key(n)	Name of the *n*-th key in storage
getItem(keyname)	Value of the *'keyname'* key
setItem(keyname,val)	Adds or modifies a couple (keyname,val)
removeItem(keyname)	Removes the *'keyname'* key
clear()	Clears the storage (makes room!)

Table 9.3. *Methods of session and permanent local storage objects*

LocalStorage performs better than cookies in size (10 MB) and in a number of properties. However, the lack of an expiration date can be an issue. It forces the user to be aware of possible memory congestion, and to empty the trash themselves[4].

9.5. Note about "JavaScript frameworks" (jQuery, D3, etc.)

Many libraries have been designed to bring additions to JavaScript. Some are built as "Module Patterns": everything is wrapped into the module's "namespace", and they are often called "frameworks". The archetype is "jQuery".

9.5.1. *A few words about jQuery*

jQuery is an open-source and multiplatform library, designed at a time when browsers were using significantly different versions of JavaScript. The first jQuery version dates back to 2006 (John Resig).

Advantages: *"write less, do more"* is the jQuery motto. Purpose: To simplify the handling of HTML DOM elements, the events and the AJAX requests. It achieves this with a single API working on all browsers, hiding

---

4 [PIL 10].

the code variations between the different versions of JavaScript: we then speak of "polyfill", hence providing a "portable code". That advantage was decisive during the 2006–2015 decade: it has greatly declined since the wide adoption of ES6.

Disadvantages: jQuery is an abstraction layer that requires additional learning, sometimes to the detriment of learning basic JavaScript: we code in jQuery more than in JavaScript. Today, jQuery looks more and more like JavaScript (with more overhead).

9.5.1.1. *Example of evolution 1: the AJAX request*

The typical AJAX request in jQuery, reading a JSON file:

```
$.ajax({
      url: url, type: 'GET', dataType: json,  //or: xml, text ...
      success: function(data) { /* code */ },
      error: function(error) { /* code for error */ }
});
```

The JavaScript equivalent, using Fetch:

```
fetch(url, { method: 'GET', mode: 'cors' })
      .then(function(res){return res.json()}) //or: .blob, .text
      .then(function(data) {/* code */ })
      .catch(function(error) { /* code for error */ });
```

9.5.1.2. *Example of evolution 2: modifying a DOM element's style*

The D3 framework proposes a service similar to jQuery:

```
d3.selectAll("p")
.style("color", "white");
```

The JavaScript equivalent is:

```
Array.from(document.querySelectorAll("p"))
.forEach(function(p){ p.style.setProperty("color", "white");});
```

9.5.2. *Recommendation*

Use the power of JavaScript, all the power of JavaScript and as far as possible only the power of JavaScript.

It is sometimes advantageous to use some features of jQuery (e.g. its user interface API for mobile) or the advanced graphics features of D3: in such cases, it is wise to isolate these pieces of code in the application.

Occam's razor states that "among competing hypotheses, the one with the fewest assumptions should be selected" (each additional library is one more assumption).

10

AJAX Technology (Asynchrony)

This chapter deals with synchronous and asynchronous processing.

Programming in the web ecosystem, that is to say, in the context the Internet, means that the speed of communication and the volume of exchanged data impact the processes. Response time can vary, and an absence of response may block a process. JavaScript is run in "single thread", hence one single blocking operation may block the whole application: we need another mechanism for creating a request and handling the return ("callback") into the event loop previously described (section 8.5).

10.1. Architecture for client–server data exchange

Dynamically adding elements in a web page traces back to 1996, with the <iframe>. In 1998, Microsoft introduced a more general solution with the ActiveX controls, then in the form of the object XMLHttpRequest in Internet Explorer. In 2005, that object was standardized by ECMA and was popularized under the name Asynchronous Javascript And XML (AJAX).

The client-side script program can post a HTTP request and then continue its activity without being blocked. When the mechanism is able to tell that an answer (or an error) is ready, the *callback* function can be run, on that response, in a similar manner to that of the processing of DOM events.

Beyond the ability to modify only part of the web page, avoiding a complete reload (including many unchanged elements), AJAX also allows access to the data files, under a variety of formats (primarily XML), served by web servers or smaller remote applications called Web Apps.

10.1.1. *The object XMLHttpRequest*

This window object is available in JavaScript, which can request XML data, as its name suggests; any text data, HTML, JSON, SVG, plain text; and also binary data (not covered here), using asynchronous HTTP GET, POST, etc. requests (the synchronous mode is not very interesting).

10.1.2. *Using XMLHttpRequest: several steps*

There are four steps in a request: (1) creating an object XMLHttpRequest, (2) opening it on a given URL in a given mode, GET or POST, (3) associating a callback function to each load and error event and (4) sending the request, possibly with data options.

We generally use a *helper* function to perform those steps, possibly in a variety of forms, depending on the request mode or the type of response expected.

10.1.2.1. *Variant "helperGetXML" (GET mode and XML expected format)*

```
function callback(error, result) {
  if (error) { throw new Error(error); }
  return processed_result;
}
function helperGetXML(url, callback, data) { // for text,
XML, HTML
  const xhr = new XMLHttpRequest();
  xhr.addEventListener("error", function() {
        callback("Http error: " + xhr.statusText);
  };
  xhr.addEventListener("load", function() {
    if (xhr.status < 400) { callback(null, xhr.responseText);
}
    else {callback("Ajax error: " + xhr.statusText);}
  };
  xhr.open("GET", url, true);    // true = asynch (default)
  xhr.setRequestHeader("Content-Type",
"text/plain;charset=utf-8");
  xhr.send(data || null);
}
```

10.1.2.2. *Variant "helperGetJSON" (GET mode, JSON expected format)*

It is mostly the same code, with a few additional specifications:

– before 'open' add the instruction:

```
xhr.overrideMimeType("application/json");
```

– inside the "onload callback", use the JSON.parse method:

```
if (xhr.status < 400) {callback(null, JSON.parse(xhr.response));}
```

Let us use it on an example:

```
const data = "param1=val1&param2=val2";   // optional data
function callbackJson(res, err) { /* process JSON object */ }
helperGetJSON(url, callbackJson, data)
```

10.2. Remarks about HTTP

– There are four request modes: GET, POST, PUT, DELETE. For accessing data, without modifying them, the mode GET is the solution for the applications targeted by this book.

– Among different possible response statuses, we probably may face only two: 200 « OK » for a success and 404 « Page not found » for all error codes are greater than or equal to 400.

10.3. "Promises" and asynchronous programming

A "Promise" is an object that represents the return (success or failure) of an async operation: it is both a container, informing on the state of the operation, and an event emitter, notifying the termination of the request. We attach "*callbacks*" to that object, rather than passing them in a function.

The use of then() is called an "*asynchronous function call*", and it returns a new "Promise" which, in turn, can be "then-ified" (chaining promises).

Approach: "callback"	Approach: "Promise"
```function success(res){ console.log("Success: "+res); } function failure(err){ console.log("Failure: "+err); } doSomething(success, failure);```	```function success(res){ console.log("Success: "+res); } function failure(err){ console.log("Failure: "+err); } doSomething() .then(success, failure);```

Table 10.1. *Comparing callback and promise mechanisms*

10.3.1. *Example: promisifying XMLHttpRequest*

We can turn `helperGetJSON` into a Promise by a simple wrapping:

```
function helperGetJson(url, data) {
   return new Promise( // anonymous version of helperGetJSON
      function (resolve, reject) {
         const xhr = new XMLHttpRequest();
         xhr.addEventListener("load", function() {
            if(this.status===200){resolve(JSON.parse(this.response));}
            else {reject(new Error('Too bad: '+this.statusText));}
         };
         xhr.addEventListener("error", function() {
            reject(new Error('Ajax Error: '+this.statusText));
         };
         xhr.overrideMimeType('application/json');
         xhr.open('GET', url);
         xhr.send(data?data:null);
   });
}
```

Let us use the promisified helper:

the method 'then' will be triggered by the notification of the termination of the request. The method accepts two functions as parameter: "resolve" and "reject" in that order:

```
helperGetJson('./file.json')
.then(
   function(value) {console.log('Contents: ' + value);},
   function(reason) {console.error('Something's wrong: ', reason);}
);
```

10.3.2. *Chaining promises*

The principle of chaining is flattening, instead of nesting:

Approach: "callback"	Approach: "Promise"
```asyncFunc1(url, function(val1) { asyncFunc2(val1, function(val2) { return ... }); })```	```asyncFunc1(url) .then(function(val1) { return asyncFunc2(); }) .then(function(val2) { ·return ... })```

Table 10.2. *Comparing callback nesting and chaining promises*

Chaining several promises is possible if the function called inside the method then returns a promise, to which another method then can be applied:

```
getPromise(url_1)                     //returns a first promise
  .then(function(data1) {
     return getPromise(url_2);        //returns a second promise
}).then(function(data)  {
     process({data1,data2});          //simple function (last one)
}).catch(function(error) {            // catches all errors
   console.log('Error occurred!', error);
});
```

The second promise must wrap the result data1 and its own result data2 into an object data = {data1,data2}, if both results are required by the function process.

10.3.3. *Parallel processing of several promises*

Any defined value can be "promisified" with this method:

```
const p = Promise.resolve([1,2,3]);
p.then(function(v) {
   // v references array [1,2,3]
});
```

We can create, for instance, a list of requests, with several helperGetJson requesting URLs from an array. These asynchronous requests, transformed into promises, can be chained by then and executed one at a time.

By using the method Promise.all, the promises are sent in parallel and results will be shown only once, when the results of all promises are received in the method all[1].

```
const urls = [ url_1, url_2 ];
const promisedUrl = urls.map(helperGetJson); // array of Promises
Promise.all(promisedUrl)       // converts the array into a Promise
.then(function(res){           // array of results (ok or error)
    res.forEach(function(text) {
        console.log(text);
    };
})
.catch(function(reason ){
    // Receives first rejection among the Promises
});
```

10.3.4. *Fetch: the promise to fetch AJAX*

The recent introduction of the object Fetch is an interesting "promise" alternative to XMLHttpRequest. We can chain directly, without having to "promisify" the helper functions.

Fetch works as follows:

```
fetch('./api/some.json')
  .then( function(res) {
      if (res.status !== 200) {
        throw new Error('problem! Status code: '+res.status);
      }
      res.json().then(function(data) {console.log(data);});
  })
  .catch(function(err) {console.log('Fetch Error :-S', err);});
```

Do note that one single catch can work for a chain of several then. We are using Fetch in several applications in Part 3.

---

1 http://exploringjs.com/es6/ch_promises.html.

10.3.5. *About the "Same Origin Policy"*

Accessing remote servers with AJAX is severely restricted for security reasons. The "Same Origin Policy" (SOP) restricts access to files present in the same domain, which means a local file, e.g. ../data/file.json.

That policy imposes that, for a document (web page) of a given origin, we cannot execute a script, coming from another origin, which tries to modify:

– window.document: any property, and no read rights on: anchors, cookie, forms, lastModified, length, links, referrer, title;

– image: lowsrc, src;

– location: all, except x and y.

There exist some means for circumventing the SOP constraint:

– <iframe>: this is old and very protective technology. Once the document is loaded in an <iframe>, it is almost impossible to access it from another element of the browser;

– "proxy" server: this must be deployed in the same domain as the files and must be programmed so that it copies data, and then these data serve the web.

– a third workaround is provided by JavaScript Object Notation with Padding (JSONP).

10.4. The exchange format: JSON

In the 1990s, standardization efforts for generalizing HTML into "eXtensible Markup Language" (XML, 1997) aimed for a generic, universal language of the Internet: XML, super-set of HTML, was a clear candidate for the universal data exchange format.

A JavaScript object literal is mere text, and can be stored as a plain text file. It was tempting to use this at least for providing data to JavaScript programs, that is to say, providing data to web pages. A data format was specified by Douglas Crockford in 2001, named "Java Script Object Notation", best known under its acronym "JSON".

Flexibility and a greater brevity are assets of JSON over XML. The object JSON was added to JavaScript, facilitating the in and out conversions, and today, most languages provide the same service.

10.4.1. *A very useful application of JSON: converting data from a spreadsheet*

We all use some spreadsheet software, either stand-alone or in the Cloud, and we all know the very simple data format called "Comma Separated Values" (CSV).

JSON is an interesting alternative to CSV: both formats can be read by most languages; CSV is certainly much more compact (the more lines in the sheet, the more advantageous), but JSON is a human readable format, and JSON can be directly embedded in JavaScript code: it is an object literal. Directly, with no transform!

Let us make comparisons with a simple example. Here is the spreadsheet:

	A	B	C	D	E	F	G	H
1	nom	prenom	age	dept	Numero	parti1	parti2	parti3
2	Dupont	Jean	22	Gironde	2	A		

and the corresponding CSV format:

```
nom, prenom, age, dept, numero, parti1, parti2, parti3
Jean, Dupont, 22, Gironde, 2, A, ,
```

It would be hard to be simpler and more compact, unless there are many empty cells, such as `parti2` and `parti3`: CSV must provide as many separated places as there are items in the first line. The other disadvantage is that compactness forces us to keep a memory of the first line, the semantic schema for each cell.

That format fits well with relational database systems, which work precisely that way: one schema plus tabulated raw data.

10.4.1.1. *The corresponding JSON format*

From the first line, we build a list of property names (keys); then, line by line, we build an object literal by picking keys from that list, and picking values in the same order from each separated value in the line, except "empty values", which are simply ignored. Hence, line 2 becomes:

```
{"nom": "Dupont", "prenom": "Jean", "Age": 22, "dept": "Gironde",
"numero": 2, "parti1": "A"}
```

Of course, it is much longer than the CSV line 2:

```
Dupont, Jean, 22, Gironde, 2, A, ,
```

but the JSON format brings other advantages:

– semantics: directly known for every line (keys);

– empty cells: their absence means undefined, e.g. l1.parti2 = undefined.

A richer structure can be derived easily:

– the properties dept and numero can be wrapped in one new object, called circo, which can be shared by all candidates in that circonscription (district):

```
{"nom": "Dupont", "prenom". "Jean", "Age": 22,
 "circo": {"dept": "Gironde", "numero": 2},
 "parti1": "A"}
```

– the properties that are in variable numbers (e.g. parti1) can be grouped into an array; the size of that array will give the number of affiliations (no need to count the non-empty values):

```
{"nom": "Dupont", "prenom": "Jean", "Age": 22,
 "circo": {"dept": "Gironde", "numero": 2},
 "affiliations": ["A"]}
```

Permanently available semantics and a rich structure, are two advantages of the JSON format at the expense of a larger memory size. Considering the number of JSON files in use in the world, these advantages are certainly important.

10.4.2. *Exporting spreadsheet data into JSON format*

In the following, we detail how to export JSON data directly from a spreadsheet using macro rules.

This takes several steps, which can be encoded as spreadsheet rules (macros).

Given a spreadsheet (e.g. `datafile.xls`):

– consider that the data are in sheet `F1`;

– use sheet 'F2' (or any) and write in cell `A1`:

```
{ "jsondata": [
```

This is the beginning of an object literal, containing a property "`jsondata`" (or any name), which opens an array literal [, to be filled by all remaining lines, down to the end. Remember that we will have to close that array and the whole object:] }.

Considering our example: the cells in use in line 1 are `'F1'!A1` to `'F1'!H1`, in line 2 (first line of data): `'F1'!A2` to `'F1'!H2`, etc.

Let us write the formula that builds the object literal for line 2. For the next lines, it will be enough to copy and drag that formula down to the last line.

The object corresponding to line 2 should be:

```
{"'F1'!A1 ":"'F1'!A2 ", "'F1'!B1 ":"'F1'!B2 ",  ... "'F1'!H1 ":"'F1'!H2 "}
```

which produces an object literal {"key1":"val1", "key2":"val2", ... }.

It is the concatenation of fixed parts (quotes, commas, colons, etc.) and cell values. Moreover, the empty values must be ignored, and we must take care of possibly conflicting quotation marks signs inside values (that is a tedious issue).

Let's start by opening the line2 object, closing it, and adding a comma if more lines are expected:

```
= CONCATENATE("{ "; [action cell A2];...; [action cell H2]; " },")
```

We must consider two cases:

– the action for cells whose value is mandatory (simple, no test);

– the action for cells which can be empty (requires a test).

WARNING 1.– In both cases, the name of the property is always in line 1 (the $ sign is needed), and its value is in the current line (no. $), for example:

```
"\"";'F1'!A$1; "\":\""; 'F1'!A2; "\""; → "nom":"Dupont".
```

WARNING 2.– The quotes for the JSON format should not conflict with those of the formula. We must escape them: "**\\"**";'F1'!A$1;   "**\\":\\"**"; 'F1'!A2;   "**\\"**";. Also: be aware of possible double-quotes inside cell values.

Therefore, the action for cells with mandatory values is the simple copy of the formula inside the CONCATENATE (note the heading comma):

```
",\"";'F1'!m$1; "\":\""; 'F1'!mi; "\"";
```

where m = [B, D, E, F], which are the four mandatory cells of our example, and i = 2, with line 2 and then all of the following lines. The heading comma is necessary for all cells, excepting the A cell (not present in our example).

The action for possibly empty cells is more complex: we must first check if it is empty, in which case we add an empty string, or otherwise, we add this concatenation formula (plus a heading comma, except with the A cell):

```
IF('F1'!mi="";""; CONCATENATE(",\""; 'F1'!m$1; "\":\""; 'F1'!mi; "\"")); 
```

where m = [A, C, G, H], the possibly empty cells of our example; i as above.

Here is the complete formula for line 2:

```
= CONCATENATE ("{ ";
 "\"";'F1'!A$1; "\":\""; 'F1'!A2; "\"";
 ", \"";  'F1'!B$1; "\":\""; 'F1'!B2; "\"";
IF('F1'!C2="";""; CONCATENATE(",\""; 'F1'!C$1; "\":\""; 'F1'!C2;
"\""));
 ", \"";  'F1'!D$1; "\":\""; 'F1'!D2; "\"";
 ", \"";  'F1'!E$1; "\":\""; 'F1'!E2; "\"";
 ", \"";  'F1'!F$1; "\":\""; 'F1'!F2; "\"";
IF('F1'!G2="";""; CONCATENATE(",\""; 'F1'!G$1; "\":\""; 'F1'!G2;
"\""));
IF('F1'!H2="";""; CONCATENATE(",\""; 'F1'!H$1; "\":\""; 'F1'!H2;
"\""));
 " },")
```

Also, we may "freeze" the column names directly in the formula, which becomes:

```
= CONCATENATE("{ ";
 "\"nom\":\""; 'F1'!A2; "\"";
 ", \"prenom\":\""; 'F1'!B2; "\"";
IF('F1'!C2=""; ""; CONCATENATE(", \"age\":\""; 'F1'!C2; "\""));
 ", \"dept\":\""; 'F1'!D2; "\"";
 ", \"numero\":\""; 'F1'!E2; "\"";
 ", \"parti1\":\""; 'F1'!F2; "\"";
IF('F1'!G2=""; ""; CONCATENATE(", \"parti2\":\""; 'F1'!G2; "\""));
IF('F1'!H2=""; ""; CONCATENATE(", \"parti3\":\""; 'F1'!H2; "\""));"
},")
```

If there are no typos, we should see the expected literal:

```
{"nom": "Dupont", "prenom": "Jean", "age": 22, "dept": "Gironde",
"numero": 2, "parti1": "A"}
```

Finally, in order to create a nested object, such as "circo", or to group properties into an array, we must arrange the necessary components. We propose this as an exercise; to pass from:

```
{"nom": "Dupont", "prenom": "Jean", "age": 22, "dept": "Gironde",
"numero": 2, "parti1": "A"}
```

to

```
{"nom": "Dupont","prenom": "Jean",    "age": 22, "circo": {"dep":
"Gironde", "num": 2}, "affiliation": ["A"]}
```

10.4.3. *Differences between JSON and the Javascript object Notation*

There are some minor differences, which we should be aware of.

– JSON accepts *only* the syntax: `"property":"string"` or `"property":number`. Double-quotes are mandatory, except for number literals;

– JSON accepted values are string, number, array, object (JSON compliant), `true`, `false`, `null` (no `undefined`);

– methods are not accepted in JSON;

– some JavaScript objects, such as Date, will be transformed into string by JSON.stringify();

– comments are forbidden in JSON. It is not a language, but a format: no engine can take care of comments. Be aware of not inserting comments in JSON files.

In conclusion, JSON is more restrictive than the JavaScript object notation. Here are some pieces of advice.

Instead of writing directly into a JSON file, follow these instructions: write the object literal, assigning it to a variable, then stringify that variable:

```
const candidat = {
        nom : "Dupont",
        prenom: 'Jean dit "Jeannot"', age : 22,
        fullName: function(){return this.prenom+" "+this.nom;}
};
console.log(JSON.stringify(candidat) );
    // -> {"nom":"Dupont","prenom":"Jean dit \"Jeannot\"","age":22}
```

The function JSON.stringify does the job for us: removing methods, adding double-quotes, possibly escaping quotes (notice the \"Jeannot\"), removing undefined properties (if any), removing spaces, tabs and line feeds.

We can directly copy the text of the datafile.json and paste it in the right-hand side of an assignment instruction:

```
const jsonText = PASTE HERE;
```
                    Do not forget the semi-colon.

More often than not, we obtain the text via an AJAX request, in which case we must use JSON.parse in the callback function: let obj = JSON.parse(response);, or response.json() if using Fetch.

NOTE.– Reading a JSON format may send warning messages to the console, complaining about bad format due to the presence of tabs, line feeds, etc. In order to avoid such warnings, we can use regular expressions and modify the input stream by adding escape characters:

```
function escapeSpecialChars(str) {
      return str.replace(/\n/g, "\\n")
                .replace(/\r/g, "\\r")
                .replace(/\t/g, "\\t")
                .replace(/\f/g, "\\f");
}
```

Finally, we are never protected against errors in the parsing of JSON data, and it is worth handling those errors by using a try.. catch:

```
function parse(str){
    try {return JSON.parse(str);}
    catch(e) {throw new Error("error in JSON parsing");}
}
```

10.5. JavaScript Object Notation with Padding

This is not a new format; it is simply the "padding" of a JSON format into an envelope. That envelope is the syntax for invoking a function f: f();. The JSON notation comes directly between the parentheses as an argument: merely an object literal notation. In an application which is possibly using several functions to read several JSONP data, it would be wise to choose the name of f in relation with the data with which we are dealing. For instance:

```
readJSONPfromX( {jsondata:[...]} );        // valid JSON expected
```

JSON file	{ "header": ["Month", "Price"], "data": [["Jan", 55.5],["Feb", 52.8], ...] }
	Ajax request on "file.json" Processing in the request's callback function

JSONP file	readJSONPfromX (
	      { "header": ["Month", "Price"],
	        "data": [["Jan", 55.5],["Feb", 52.8], ...]
	      }
	);

	<script src="main.js"></script> must contain readJSONPfromX Request by <script src="file.jsonp"></script> Immediate invocation of the function readJSONPfromX

Table 10.3. *Comparing how to read JSON and JSONP data*

The function readJSONPfromX must have been previously defined in the application before accessing the JSONP. Be aware of the order of operations.

The JSONP file is read as mere text by the engine, and then comes the interpretation as JavaScript code, compounding only one instruction. That instruction invokes a function; if the function is defined, it is executed with the literal object as argument.

```
<script src= "main.js"></script>
<script src= "https://url_du_fichier/file.jsonp"></script>
```

This choice provides the important advantage to avoid the SOP constraint. It presents a security risk, the same as when using any unreliable script. Preferably use JSONP data provided by secure "https" sites.

10.6. A parallel JavaScript: the "worker"

The client-side JavaScript is single threaded (one per window). Since the introduction of "web workers" in HTML5, we can run a script (or a few) in the background, on another thread independent of any user interface.

Below, we have the example of a dialog between DOM events and a worker. Here is the code[2] of the main JavaScript:

```
const first = document.querySelector('#number1'),
      second = document.querySelector('#number2'),
      result = document.querySelector('.result');
const myW = new Worker("worker.js"); //external script
first.onchange = function() {        // a value has changed
      myW.postMessage([first.value,second.value]); // [message]
      console.log('to worker');                          // 8
};
second.onchange = function() {
      myW.postMessage([first.value,second.value]);
      console.log('to worker');                          // 12
};
myW.onmessage = function(e) {
      result.textContent = e.data;
      console.log('from worker');                        // 16
};
```

---

2 http://mdn.github.io/simple-web-worker/.

The code in the external file 'worker.js' is:

```
onmessage = function(e) {
  console.log('from main');                          // 2
  let workerResult = 'Result: ' + (e.data[0] * e.data[1]);
  console.log('to main '+workerResult);              // 4
  postMessage(workerResult);
};
```

Do note that the worker has access to some resources of the `window` object, as it can use the `console`. But the worker does not have access to the DOM.

Here is the dialog between the two processes:

Text on DOM	Text on `console`	Thread:line
to worker		Main:8
	from main	worker.js:2
	to main	worker.js:4
from worker		Main:16
to worker		Main:12
	from main	worker.js:2
	to main	worker.js:4
from worker		Main:16

Table 10.4. *Example of a dialog with a worker*

Applications

Introduction to Part 3

Let us talk about *"Big Data"*: not about a *Big Bang* or a *Big Brother* myth, but merely about a big reservoir of data, of any kind, which we can examine under two facets:

– we can consider the *Big* facet, when billions of data concern a particular topics, which we can process through distributed statistical processing or deep learning.

– we can consider the *Data* facet, meaning that we can gather information pieces about almost anything, without being constrained by performance issues.

Our approach focuses rather on that second facet, in particular on the servers that deliver data that can be accessed through APIs, or JSONP, or even plain text files such as CSV data, or loosely structured data such as RSS feeds.

Being able to process such data requires different skills:

– accessing several resources: monitoring AJAX requests and responses;

– aggregating data, joining data (SQL like GroupBy and Join);

– displaying graphs, plotting curves, animating;

– mapping data on cartographic sources, map-data interactions.

The first application works on temporal data series. We will put in practice the AJAX technology, the array methods, the canvas graphic tools and animation tools.

The second application deals with multiple tabulated data sources in relational or hierarchical mode. We will present an operation similar to GroupBy and Join; we will face string comparison issues and use the prototypal background of JavaScript for a smooth integration of JSON data. Performance can be an issue in such applications and we will discuss Javascript "promises".

The next application domain is cartography and we will explore the two main modes: SVG- and canvas-based APIs.

Finally, we will present three examples of using data services using JSONP: accessing spreadsheets, image catalogs and RSS feeds.

Chronological Data

11.1. Accessing a JSON file via AJAX

This example is characteristic of many sites that provide access to chronological data, generally under CSV and JSON formats.

Quandl.com is a data warehouse which basically sells financial data. It also gives free access to economic and demographic data, mostly from public sources such as the World Bank, the European Central Bank (ECB), Euronext and the French office of statistics INSEE or from universities such as Yale Department of Economics and Paris School of Economics.

11.1.1. *Quick presentation of the Quandl API*

The directory `https://www.quandl.com/api/v3/datasets/` gives direct access to JSON formatted data with the following command:

```
GET
https://www.quandl.com/api/v3/datasets/{db_code}/{data_code}.json
```

db_code	data_code
PSE **(Paris school of economics)**	USA_1010120401 (Top 0.5-0.1% income share - USA, excluding capital gains)
INSEE	63_001686811_A (Population of 60+ years in France - mainland)

Table 11.1. *Example of data from the Quandl.com catalog*

The JSON data structure is normalized as in this example (excerpts):

```
{
  "dataset": {
    "name":"World Top Incomes - Top 0.5-0.1% income share - United States",
    "description":"Units=%. Fractiles: total income excl. capital gains",
    "column_names": [ "Date", "Value" ],
    "frequency": "annual",
    "start_date": "1913-12-31",
    "end_date": "2015-12-31",
    "data": [ [ "2015-12-31", 6.29 ], ... ]
  }
}
```

11.1.2. *Processing an example with promises*

Knowing that structure and the components of the URL, we are able to write a *callback* function and call the helperGetJson function (presented in Chapter 10) with the correct arguments (url and no data).

```
const db = "PSE/", ds = "USA_1010120401";
const key = "a_key_provided_by_quandl"; //no key: limit 50 req.
const url = "https://www.quandl.com/api/v3/datasets/"+db+ds+
".json?api_key="+key;
fetch(url)                        // returns 1st promise
  .then(res => res.json())    // returns 2nd promise
  .then(processQuandl)         // achieves final processing
  .catch(function(err){console.log('Fetch Error:-S', err);});
```

First, we build the url that refers the particular database (PSE) and dataset that we want to process. The api_key can be omitted but there is a 50 request limit in that case.

Then we use fetch to send the query and return a first promise, which we convert into JSON, and it returns a second promise, which we finally use in this function:

```
function processQuandl(response){
  const set = response.dataset;
  const getShare = (t)=> t[1];        // the second array gives %
  const getYear = (t)=> parseInt(t[0].substring(0,4)); // year
  const initCurve = function(title,color){/* code presented */}
  const drawCurve = function(time,val){/* in section graphics */}
  let title = set.name +` [${set.start_date} - ${set.end_date}]`;
  let rev = set.data.reverse();        // for ascending time
  initCurve(title, "green");
```

```
drawCurve(rev.map(getYear), rev.map(getShare));
  // then we can overlay some events such as presidency terms
  // putEvents(president, data);  // see: 'additional data'
return res; // we can return a promise, if we want a next 'then'
}
```

Chronological data that are delivered as JSON can be directly received as JavaScript objects presenting similar properties:

– metadata: such as a name, a date or a period (start-end dates);

– data: a 2D array i.e. an array of arrays (all inner arrays containing two elements), t = [[date, value], ...].

The array can be used for plotting the curve y = value(date), because the relation between date and value is functional (one value per date). The functions getYear and getShare provide the abscissa and ordinate respectively, by mapping separately the date and the value into two new arrays (method map). Then these arrays are passed in arguments to the function drawCurve, already detailed in chapter 9, and the function initCurve prepares the canvas and initializes some geometric values. The functions initCurve and drawCurve can be replaced by equivalent functions taken from some graphic library but the overall logic of the application is the same.

11.1.2.1. Additional data

The historical data from that example spans over a century, from 1913 to 2015, and concerns the share of GDP owned by the most wealthy people (0.5% uppermost revenues). In order to relate these data to some historical events, we can search for the presidential terms of the President of the United States during that century.

Here are the data:

```
const president = [
    ["1913-1921",8,"T. Woodrow Wilson","D"], ["1921-1923",2,"Warren G. Harding","R"],
    ["1923-1929",6,"J. Calvin Coolidge","R"], ["1929-1933",4,"Herbet C. Hoover","R"],
    ["1933-1945",12,"Franklin D. Roosevelt","D"], ["1945-1953",8,"Harry S. Truman","D"],
    ["1953-1961",8,"Dwight D. Eisenhower","R"], ["1961-1963",2,"John F. Kennedy","D"],
    ["1963-1969",6,"Lyndon B. Johnson","D"], ["1969-1974",5,"Richard M. Nixon","R"],
    ["1974-1977",3,"Gerald R. Ford","R"], ["1977-1981",4,"Jimmy Carter","D"],
    ["1981-1989",8,"Ronald Reagan","R"], ["1989-1993",4,"George H. W. Bush","R"],
    ["1993-2001",8,"Bill Clinton","D"], ["2001-2009",8,"George W. Bush","R"],
    ["2009-2017",8,"Barack Obama","D"]
];
```

This function uses some <div> elements, whose creation and setting are not described here:

```
function putEvents(table, datab) {
        // Color according to President's party
  let Dgd = "linear-gradient(to bottom,#99ccff 64%,#0000ff 100%)";
  let Rgd = "linear-gradient(to bottom,#ff99cc 66%,#ff0000 100%)";
  let date0 = parseInt(table[0][0].substring(0,4));
  table.forEach(function(tp, p, tab){
  // display a coloured <div> spanning over the President's term
  div.addEventListener("mouseover",function(e) {
    // coding data to popup
  });
}
```

With the help of some CSS rules for coloring the elements, we present here the graphical output.

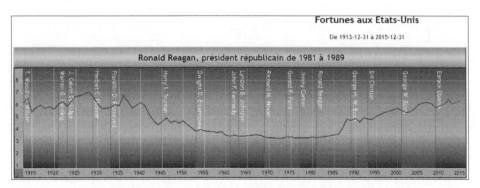

Figure 11.1. *Plot of chronological data from Json file and overlays*

This kind of application does not require a deep understanding of all the facets of JavaScript. It is within the reach of a secondary school teacher, with the contribution of students and a minimum equipment.

EXERCISE.–

Use the same code with the second example (INSEE demographic data of people 60+ years in France, over the same century). Instead of raw data, display the annual %-change: rev[i] $\rightarrow$ (rev[i] - rev[i-1])/rev[i-1] (the first value rev[0] cannot be computed).

Then, for each important variation, find which event occurred 60 years earlier; that is easy and impressive.

11.2. Using open source graphic libraries

We already mentioned some of the graphic tools[1] that propose to handle graphical data under different classical forms: line-chart, pie-chart, Gantt-chart, etc.

Once we have learnt the basic mechanisms, it is easier to work with the features of such libraries. Hereafter, we detail how to use the library dygraph.js for:

– plotting several chronological data relative to the same abscissa axis;

– animating chronological data against time.

11.2.1. *Plot multiple data series against the same time axis*

This is a typical example of the different steps to achieve:

– extract the data from the source;

– convert CSV into JSON. In this example, the ECB SDMX 2.1 RESTful web service, operational since 2017, provides an API for accessing the ECB Statistical Data Warehouse;

– reverse the array (ascending time);

– convert dates into JavaScript Date objects (goodDate);

– set labels and format axes;

Here is the code (Ajax request not repeated):

```
const ecbTGB = {
    "name":"Euro TARGET balance (selected countries)",
    "dataSource": "http://sdw.ecb.europa.eu/browse.do?node=bbn4859",
    "Unit": "[Millions of Euro]",
    "Participants": ["ECB","BE","DE","ES","FR","IT","NL"],
```

---

1 See http://www.datasciencecentral.com/profiles/blogs/8-free-popular-javascript-charting-libraries.

```
  "data": [
    ["2017Aug",-212940,-22095,852511,-384426,9278,-414164,107511],
    [...], ... ]
}
const dygrafTable = ecbTGB.data.reverse(); // latest right
function goodDate(x){
    let xx = x[0], y = parseInt(xx);
    x[0] = new Date( xx.split(y)[1]+" 1 "+y );
    return x;
}
dygrafTable = dataTable.map(goodDate);
const dygrafDiv = document.querySelector(".plot");
let title = ecbTGB.name, width = 480, height = 200;
let labels = ['Date'].concat(source.Participants);
let axes = {x:{pixelsPerLabel: 30,
               axisLabelFormatter(x){return x.getFullYear();}
          };
const g = new Dygraph(
    dygrafDiv ,              // where to plot
    dygrafTable,             // data (or url to a CSV file
    {title, width, height, labels, axes}
);
```

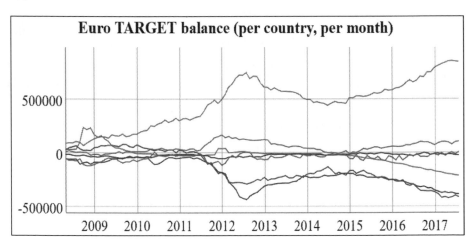

Figure 11.2. *Multiple chronological data series (several countries)*

11.2.2. *Dynamic plot: simulating time evolution*

The plot is displayed on the screen in just one frame. We may want to control that display by using as many frames as needed, to simulate an evolution, for example, at the pace of 1 s per year:

– first, we draw only the first date (2008), as in the previous example;

– we create a function that adds the next date (push) and we call the updateOptions method of the object Dygraph (it forces frame refresh);

– we invoke window.setInterval, which repeats that every ms milliseconds;

– we stop (clearInterval) when the maximal size is reached.

Except updateOptions, which is Dygraph specific, the logic is general to any similar animation (to control the speed of a plot). Here is the code:

```
const dynamicTable = Array.from([dygrafTable[0]]);  // = 2008
const maxlen = dygrafTable.length;  // stop test
function dynamicDraw(){
    dynamicTable.push(dygrafTable[dynamicTable.length]);
    if(dynamicTable.length === maxlen)
        clearInterval(window.intervalId);
    g.updateOptions( {'file':dynamicTable} );
}
let ms = 500; // every 500 ms
window.intervalId = setInterval(dynamicDraw, ms);
```

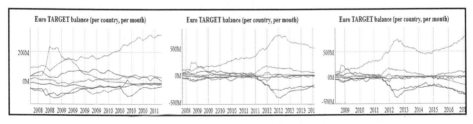

Figure 11.3. *Successive plots, after 2 s (2011), 4 s (2014) and 6 s (2017)*

In the example, the interval of the vertical axis adapts itself to the range of the values read so far. We can notice an important scale change around the year 2010 (after 2.5 s): interval [-150M, 200M] becomes [-500M, 500M].

12

Relational Data

We consider in this chapter, the simplest and most popular form of relational data and tabulated data. There exists billions of spreadsheets data, either from Excel, or from other software. Also, data from RDBMS (relational database management systems) can be easily exported as tabulated data, for instance under a "comma separated values" (CSV) format, or, as we have already learned, in JSON files.

Let us detail two important operations that can be done with a simple browser: data aggregation and data join.

12.1. Aggregating tabulated JSON data

The relational nature of tabulated data does not fit well with hierarchical structures, which introduce that which is called "dimensions", for instance, the spatial dimension of an administrative breakdown or the taxonomic dimension of the scientific classification of the living beings.

This is well-known in database management systems, and data warehouses frequently use the joins and aggregators to pass from relational to hierarchical representations of the same datasets. At the browser scale, we are facing similar issues, and we must realize operations similar to Sql Left Join or Sql GroupBy, between data coming from several JSON files. We describe these processing with the JavaScript code of the following example: the analysis of electoral data.

12.1.1. *Electoral data: administrative breakdown, political breakdown*

The administrative breakdown is a well-known issue. In France, there are five levels: [communes], [circonscriptions], [departement], [region] and [France].

The inclusion relation is transitive, which is easy to handle, but does not exist between communes and circonscriptions: a few large communes are split between several circonscriptions, alone, or together with other smaller communes.

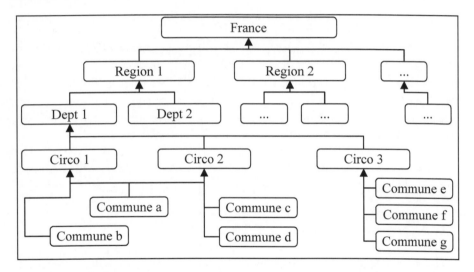

Figure 12.1. *Breaking down the "spatial dimension" of the electoral application*

In the same way, political affinities may make it so that some candidates declare several "labels". The dimension "*affiliation*" compounds have two levels: label and group.

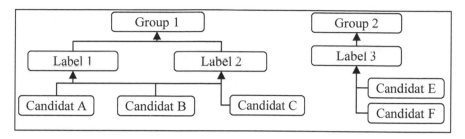

Figure 12.2. *Breaking down the "affiliation dimension" of the electoral application*

The non-functional nature of such breakdowns is the source of some issues. For instance, the cumulation of votes by department (or a higher level) can lead to a total lower than the total of the votes, if we cumulate by "first label" (some missing), or to a superior total if we cumulate by "group" (some duplicates). The cross between the two dimensions is at the level: Candidat ↔ Circonscription.

Therefore, the two basic objects are as follows:

– the "candidat" (candidate), which determines a unique "circonscription" (hence a "department") and which owns a list of political labels;

– the "circonscription" (constituency), which maintains the list of its *candidats* and where votes, spread over the "communes", must be cumulated.

There are some other objects as follows:

– the *departement*, which is a list of one or more *circonscriptions*: cumulating votes by party label is sometimes an issue (see later);

– regions and full France: same counting issues;

– *groups*: observed from ahead of vote declarations and on election day.

The sources of data concern the election of the member of the French Assemblée nationale during the 2017 election ("législatives").

Available data about the candidates, the circonscriptions and the vote
Candidate's declarations: political and financial affiliation
https://www.interieur.gouv.fr/Elections/Elections-legislatives-2017/Declaration-de-rattachement-a-un-parti-ou-groupement-politique
https://www.interieur.gouv.fr/Elections/Elections-legislatives-2017/Elections-legislatives-le-financement-public-des-partis-politiques2
Results by commune
https://www.data.gouv.fr/fr/datasets/elections-legislatives-des-11-et-18-juin-2017-resultats-du-2nd-tour-par-communes
Commune-level INSEE data
https://public.opendatasoft.com/explore/dataset/correspondance-code-insee-code-postal/api/?

Table 12.1. *List of the data sources used in the electoral application*

12.1.1.1. *Accessing JSON-formatted data*

Let us start with the most voluminous dataset, results and then declarations:

– R-data: results of the first round ("élections législatives 2017") and resulting from a spreadsheet transformed into this JSON format:

```
{ data: [
  {dn:#Dept, dl:NomD, c:NumCirco, cn:#Commune, cl:NomC,
   i:Registered, v:Voting, b:WhiteVotes, n:NullVotes,
   can:[{s:Sex, n:Lastnama, p:Fist, g:Label, v:Votes}, ...]},
  {...}
]}
```

Here is a sample line:

```
{"dn":1, "dl":"Ain", "c":1, "cn":16, "cl":"Arbigny", "i":317, "v":157,
 "b":10, "n":1,"can":[{"s":"M", "n":"MALLET", "p":"Laurent", "g":"MDM",
 "v":12},{"s":"M", "n":"NOM2", "p":"Prénom2", "g":"ET2", "v":21}, ... ]},
```

– D-data: data from forms filled in by candidates before the registration deadline (about 2 weeks before election day). Some late candidacies are not listed, and some candidates did not provide ballots on election day. Several candidates have filled two or three different affiliations.

Here is a sample line, before and after the processing that breaks down the single string into a meaningful object:

```
{"Ain*1e_circo*M*MALLET Laurent 15/06/1972 MODEM"}
{dep:"Ain",c:1,s:"M",n:"MALLET",p:"Laurent",dob:"15/06/1972",g:"MODEM"}
```

12.1.2. *Aggregating data along the spatial dimension: votes by circonscription*

In a relational database, this operation could have been done "à la SQL", with the aggregator sum and the operator GroupBy:

```
SELECT SUM(votes), Candidat
FROM Communes
WHERE Departement = "D" AND Circonscription = "C"
GROUP BY Candidat;
```

Here is the JavaScript code for aggregating data from each *commune* of each *circonscription* of each *departement*, resulting in an array indexed by *departement*:

```
function processRdata(json){
// @json. {'data':[line1, line2, ...]}
// line = {dn, dl, c, cn, cl, i, v, b, n, can:[{s,n,p,g,v},...]}
  const dept = [];   // will be updated every makeNewDepartement
  let curDep = null, curCir = null;
  function processRline(line, i){   // code pour chaque ligne
    let ldn = line.dn.toString(), lci = line.c;
    if(curDep && curDep.num === ldn){      // dep exists and is ok
      if(lci === curDep.circos.length){ curCir.update(line);
      }else{
        curCir = makeNewCirconscription(line); // new circo in dep
        curDep.addCirco(curCir);
      }
    }else{
      curDep = makeNewDepartement(line,dept);   // new dep
      curCir = makeNewCirconscription(line);      // new circo
      curDep.addCirco(curCir);             // add to dep
    }
  }
  json.data.forEach(processRline);          // loop on lines
  return dept;
}
```

NOTE.– The code makes the assumption that data are sequentially listed by circonscription and by department, not randomly. It simplifies the test using the current number curCir or curDep (linear rather than exponential search).

Here are the functions for creating a *departement* and a *circonscription*:

```
function makeNewDepartement(dat, depts){
  let num = dat.dn.toString(), nom = dat.dl;
  let rank = department.length, circos = [];
  let dept = Object.assign(Object.create(depProto),
                           {num, nom, rank, circos});
  depts.push(dept);
  return dept;
}
function makeNewCirconscription(dat){
  let circ = null;
  delete dat.cn; delete dat.cl;              // unused properties
  dat.can = dat.can.map(function(x){  // can update
    x.dn = this.dn.toString(); x.c = this.c;  // see: NOTE below
    x.partis = [x.g];
    return Object.assign(Object.create(canProto), x);
  },dat);
  circ = Object.assign(Object.create(cirProto), dat);
  return circ;
}
const depProto = Departement.prototype,
      cirProto = Circonscription.prototype,
      canProto = Candidat.prototype;
```

In that code, the same line of data dat is used for the creation of both the *departement* and the *circonscription*. Using the method map avoids using a loop. Also, we are using the assign/create pattern that allows the creation of an object benefiting from the methods of depProto and the properties {num, nom, rank, circos} adapted from dat. The creation of the *departement* also fills in the array provided by the calling function processRline.

The same assign/create pattern is used for creating a *circonscription*, this time using cirProto as prototype. Regarding the creation of each *candidat* in the list of candidates of that circonscription, note that it is done once, using canProto, for the first commune of the circonscription. The next lines of the same circonscription will only update the number of votes. The line of data can be used directly (no adaptation) in the assign method, but we can delete some useless properties (name and number of each *commune*)

```
delete dat.cn; delete dat.cl;           // unused properties
```

NOTE.– The assign/create pattern uses the flexibility of the prototypal approach and is efficient in lines of code, as it simply reuses fragments of the JSON data.

We may notice the use of the method map, with its optional second parameter, which allows us to bind the value of the pronoun this:

```
dat.can = dat.can.map(function(x){
    x.dn = this.dn.toString(); x.c = this.c;
    x.partis = [x.g];
    return Object.assign(Object.create(canProto), x);
}, dat);                // option: binds 'this' to dat
```

The reason is that we need dat.dn and dat.c inside the callback of a map method applied on the array can: the solution of binding this is very convenient.

12.1.3. *Aggregating data along the affiliations dimension: labels by candidate*

In order to get the multiple affiliations (at least one) of a candidate, we require a kind of auto-join with a concatenation aggregator somewhat similar to:

```
SELECT DISTINCT d1.Candidat, CONCAT(d1.Parti, d2.Parti)
FROM Depots AS d1
WHERE d1.Departement = "D" AND d1.Circonscription = "C"
    LEFT OUTER JOIN Depots AS d2
                ON d1.Departement = "D" AND d1.Circonscription = "C"
                        AND d2.Candidat = d1.Candidat
GOUP BY Candidat
HAVING d1.Parti <> d2.Parti
```

The JavaScript code is a bit more complex than processRdata:

```
function processDdata(json){
// @json: {'data':[line1, line2, ...]}
// line = {string} to be transformed in {dep, c, s, n, p, dob, g}
```

```
  const declared = [], multiaff = [];
  let curCan = null;
  const processDline = function (line, i){/*see below*/};
  json.data.forEach(processDline);
  return {declared, multiaff};
}
```

It returns an object made up of two arrays: the full list of "declared" candidates, and the list of candidates having filled in more than one affiliation. The code for the per line function is:

```
function processDline(line, i){
  let can = makeCandidatFromD(line); // pre-process, see below
  if(!can.dob){return false;} // no declaration yet in circo
  if(curCan){
    if(curCan.isSame(can)){  // groupBy -> aggegate parties
      curCan.aggregate(can); // same name expected to follow
      if(!multiple.some(x => x.isSame(curCan))){
          multiple.push(curCan); // if not a duplicate, keep it
      }
      return false;          // proceed with groupBy
    }else {                  // else: this is a new candidat
      declared.push(curCan); // store previous aggregated cand.
    }
  }    // now set or reset curCan
  curCan =
Object.assign(Object.create(canProto),can,{partis:[can.g]});
  return this;
}
```

NOTE.– The code is simplified under the assumption that multiple declarations of a same candidate are in sequence (which is the case), which eases to reduce them into one single array entry. The assign/create pattern is used again with canProto and a direct copy of can. One more property partis is added directly within the assign method call.

The function makeCandidatFromD uses features described in Chapter 3:

```
function makeCandidatFromD(original){
  const spl = original.split("*"); // separator * > array 2+ items
  const foundDate = str => str.match(/ \d\d.\d\d.\d\d\d\d /);
  let dep = spl[0], c = parseInt(spl[1]);       // tr.: "1e_circo" -> 1
  if(spl.length>3){
    const ok = foundDate(spl[3]);
    if(ok){                             // ok = a date has been found
```

```
      const newx = spl[3].split(ok); // split before/after date
      const name = newx[0];
      const spn = name.split(" ");
      const s = spl[2];
      const n = spn.reduce((n,s,i) => n + (s.toUpperCase()===s?
                                           (i>0?" ":"")+s:"") );
      const p = unAccentize(name.slice(n.length+1, name.length));
      const dob = ok[0].substring(1, 11); // separator is the date
      const g = unAccentize(newx[1]);
        return {dep, c, s, n, p, dob, g};
    }
  }
  return {dep, c}; // just a dummy candidat (should have one)
}
```

12.2. Joining data: multiple JSON files

Combining several sources of information is a fundamental operation for a *data scientist*. For a join to be possible, it requires that the two sources have at least one common ground to allow an association. The difficulty could be to determine such a "key", and how the key is "joinable". By "joinable" we mean: do we need an exact value equality between the keys, or the membership to a same equivalence class, or some more fuzzy association, allowing possible multiple associations?

We will not talk about sophisticated AI algorithms, but merely string processing: for instance, to accept *"Général de Gaule"* as well as *"general de Gaulle"*.

12.2.1. *Advantage of the flexibility brought by the prototypal approach*

The flexibility that we may expect when processing a join can take advantage of the flexibility of the assign/create pattern. One prototype can be shared by several objects that only own a subset of common properties. The polymorphism of the processing, according to the number of sources actually used, without an *a priori* knowledge of how many would be available, is another advantage of the prototypal approach.

Here is an example with the D-data (declarations), which allows us to build a *candidat* with the properties {sex, lastname, first, dob, aff: [p1,p2..]}, and with the R-data (official results), which allows us to build an actual *candidat*, with properties: {sex, lastname, first, party, votes}.

The prototypal approach cares only about the existing properties, and we can give the same prototype to an R-based candidat and to a D-based candidat, provided that enough properties are set. For instance, the test if(can.dob && !can.v) informs us about the status of can: if true, it means that can has been initialized from D-data, and has not yet been updated with additional R-data.

12.2.2. *Coding the join on the electoral application*

The basic object to join is the *candidat*, however, the data are hierarchized from *departement*, to *circonscription*, then finally to *candidat*. Therefore, we need to make a joinability test to each three levels. Here is the code for the method isSame in each of the prototypes:

– *departement*: it is encoded differently in R-data or D-data, the name of the already processed department is this.nom, and the name of the not yet processed one (in dat) can be dat.dep or dat.dl, depending on the second source. Here is the polyfill using the acceptString function detailed below:

```
Departement.prototype.isSame = function(dat){  // polyfill
   const str = ("dep" in dat)? dat.dep: (("dl" in dat)?dat.dl:dat);
   return acceptString(this.nom, str);
};
```

– *circonscription*: just check the number (same encoding)

```
Circonscription.prototype.isSame = function(dat){return this.c ===
dat.c;};
```

– candidat:

```
Candidat.prototype.isSame = function(dat){
   return acceptString(this.n,dat.n) && acceptString(this.p,dat.p);
};
```

The function acceptString compares two strings and accepts strings without caring about uppercase versus lowercase, or accentuated versus non-accentuated letters, also ignoring hyphen versus whitespace ("Côte-d'Or" accepted as "Cote d'or").

Here is the code for the join (R-data are updated with D-data):

```
function join(dept,decla){
//@dept: list of departments built by processRdata
//@decla: list of declared candidates, built by processDdata
   let lenR = dept.length, lenD = declares.length,
       curNDep = 0, curNCir = 0;
   const joinDtoRdata = function(can){ // merges D-data to R-data
     // @can = one aggregated "D-based" candidat
     let dep = dept[curNDep], cir;
     while(!dep.isSame(can)){ // seeks for the right dep
       curNDep++; dep = dept[curNDep]; curNCir = 0;
     }
     if(dep) cir = dep.circos[curNCir];
     else throw new Error("join: no Dept for "+can.dep+""+can.c);
     while(cir && !cir.isSame(can)){
       curNCir++; cir = dep.circos[curNCir];
     }
     if(cir) cir.crossUpdate(can);
     else throw new Error("join: no Circo for "+can.dep+""+can.c);
   };
   if(lenD > 0){declares.forEach(joinDtoRdata);}
   return {dept:dept, declares:decla};
}
```

Here is the code for the method crossUpdate (*circonscription* and *candidat* levels):

```
Circonscription.prototype.crossUpdate = function(dat){
   let dd = this.can.find(function(x){return x.isSame(dat);});
   if(dd){dd.crossUpdate(dat);}
   else{disparus.push(dat);} // if we want to keep track of them
};
Candidat.prototype.crossUpdate = function(dat){// update R from D
   this.partis = this.partis.concat(dat.partis);
   this.dob = dat.dob;
   return this;
};
```

NOTE.– A *circonscription* may count more than 100 *communes* and there may be up to 25 *candidats* in some *circonscriptions*. France counts 577 *circonscriptions*. Such a volume of data imposes a careful coding, aware of performance issues (memory and speed). We will see how to chain the whole processing in order not to hamper the display of the results.

12.3. Postprocessing: analysis

Once the operations GroupBy, by data source, and join between aggregated results are achieved, one can design a series analysis processing, akin to Select (element) from (array) Where (element meets criterion).

Here is a simple example: count the total votes in France:

```
let totvot = depts.reduce(    //@depts: computed from joinDtoR
    function(tot, d){
      return tot + d.circos.reduce(
        function(count, c){ return count + c.v;}, 0);
    },
    0)
);
```

or in arrow syntax version:

```
let totvot = depts
  .reduce((tv,d) => tv + d.circos.reduce((t,c) => t + c.v, 0),0);
printLog("Nb total de votants "+ totvot );
```

Again we note that the `Array.prototype` methods are very convenient.

12.3.1. *Analyzing the affiliations*

The partisan affiliations are not necessarily the names of usual political parties, but groups that accept to share the management of financial contributions. On election day, the authorities (the French *Ministère de l'Interieur*) give their own label for candidates. There are many "undecided" candidates, with the label "DIV" ("diverse"), sometimes "DVG" or "DVD", meaning a "diverse" leaning left or right.

In order to better know what these affiliation groups are, we take an example:

```
const text = "CAISSE CLAIRE";
const crit = function(p){return p.includes(text);};
let gp = [];                    // expected: an array of candidat
depts.forEach(function(d){      // departement d
  d.circos.forEach(function(c){      // circonscription c
    gp = gp.concat(c.can.filter(
        function(x){            // candidat x
                    return x.partis.some(crit);
            }                   // apply crit on x.partis
    ));                         // filter candidats then concat
  });                          // by circonscription
});                            // by departement
```

The arrow syntax is more readable:

```
depts.forEach(function(d){
  d.circos.forEach(function(c){
    gp = gp.concat(c.can.filter((x)=> x.partis.some(crit)));
  });
});
```

The result is the concatenation for each *circonscription* of each *departement* of the list of the *candidat*s affiliated to the given group. For instance, "CAISSE CLAIRE" has 105 candidates, of which 76 are labeled as DIV by the authorities, 15 as DVG (leaning left), six as DVD (leaning right), seven as ECO (ecologist) and one as REG (regionalist). They are very diverse and got 50,972 votes nationwide.

12.4. The role of promises

The R-data electoral results are voluminous: 30 Mega, D-data: only 500 k. The interest of using *promises* is to allow the asynchronous processing of each file, before processing the join and then the postprocessing. We know how to use Fetch on a JSON file, and we have learned how to write a closure that transforms any function into a promise.

Consider this example about the second step only (D-data processing):

```
function step2(url,dept,json){              // synchronous version
  let decla = processDdata(json)
```

```
  if (decla.length > 0) {resolve(decla,dept);}
  else reject(url); // error message on url
}
function step2Promise(url,dept,json){        // "promise" version
  return new Promise(function(resolve, reject) {
    let decla = processDdata(json);
    if (decla.length > 0) {resolve(decla,dept);}
    else throw new Error("failure with "+url); // or: reject()
  });
}
```

The overall chain of processes may look like the following code: the function resolve is the first argument of the next call to then. Handling errors may use the second argument (optional function reject), or, as in this code, merely throw an error that will be processed asynchronously by a single catch for the whole chain.

```
const url_R = "fileR.json";
const url_D = "fileD.json";
fetch(url_R)
    .then(a => a.json().then(jsonR => [a.url,jsonR]))
    .then(([urlR,jsonR]) => step1(urlR,jsonR))
    .then(([dept]) => fetch(url_D)
                    .then(d => d.json()
                            .then(jsonD => [d.url,dept,jsonD])))
    .then(([urlD,dept,jsonD]) => step2(urlD, dept, jsonD) )
    .then(([dept,decla]) =>
            {let res = step3(decla,dept); step4(res);}
    )
    .catch(reason => printLogAndStatus("error caught: "+reason));
```

That code needs some explanations:

– we start with a fetch request on the first file, which returns a promise that we must first read with the JSON method, which, in turn, returns a new promise. We may treat that promise directly with step 1, but we want to forward a second argument (here: just the name of the file), therefore, we must use a second function to wrap the promise and that argument: it is the role of the function jsonR => [a.url,jsonR];

– the next line: .then(([urlR,jsonR]) => step1(urlR,jsonR)) processes the result (the "resolved" promise) with step1. The scripting ([urlR,jsonR]) clearly shows the components of the result, but we can use a simple object to wrap them together, and let function step 1 to decompose that object in its two components;

– the next line is a bit more complex: the dept array must be passed through the intermediate processing (a fetch(), followed by a json()), because we need it in the sequel. Therefore, the promise sequence fetch+json must be wrapped with the dept array, in a similar way as the promise of the first fetch call;

– next line: processes the resolved promise with step 2, the function that we detailed above;

– and finally, we can apply the join step3 and the postprocessing step4. We may also promisify step 3 if some asynchronous resource would have been required, for instance the socioeconomic data from the INSEE source.

12.4.1. *Performance considerations with the electoral application*

Within each of the six steps, the code is framed between two calls to a function giving the real elapsed time in milliseconds:

```
function printLogAndStatus(message) { // t0 a control variable
    t0 = (window.performance.now() - t0),
    console.log(message +". In "+t0.toFixed(0)+" ms.");
}
```

Logs	Action	(ms)
Promesse tenue ./Ddata.json: Ajax ok 300 ms.	→Reading, parsing file 1	300
Resultat GroupBy (107 items). En 737 ms.	→step1: groupBy on source 1	737
Promesse tenue ./Rdata.json: Ajax ok 338 ms.	→Reading parsing file 2	338
Resultat GroupBy (6790 items). En 1290 ms.	→step2: groupBy on source 2	1,290
Jointure des R-data et D-data. En 1116 ms.	→Joint 2 sources	1,116
Calculs et affichages. En 2221 ms.	→Analysis and display	2,221

Table 12.2. *The six steps in the promisified version of the application*

12.5. Using Google Gantt chart for a graphic visualization

The six asynchronous steps of the chain can be visualized with the help of a *Gantt chart*, a relevant tool for the management of asynchronous tasks.

We can use the Google chart API, which creates SVG-based graphics, and which has a *Gantt* module. We must use the Google loader:

```
<script src="https://www.gstatic.com/charts/loader.js"></script>
```

Here is the code that we can use in the *handler* of the *domLoaded* event:

```
// list of required data for computing the "Gantt"
let taskID, taskName, start, end, duration, donePercent, after;
const rows = [                    // the 6 steps
    ['D', 'declarations', new Date(), null, 300, 0, ''],
    ['E', 'decGroupBy', null, null,  737), 0, 'D'],
    ['R', 'resultats', null, null,  338,  0, ''],
    ['S', 'resGroupBy', null, null, 1290, 0, 'R'],
    ['J', 'Join(res,dec)', null, null, 1116, 100, 'S,E'],
    ['A', 'Analyse', null, null,  2221, 100, 'J'] ];
// Load the API with the gantt package, then set a callback
const googleDiv = document.querySelector("#chart_div");
google.charts.load('current', {'packages':['gantt']});
google.charts.setOnLoadCallback(drawChart);
const msPerD = (days)=> parseInt(days* 24* 60* 60* 1000);
const getTyp = (v)=> v===null||v instanceof Date?'date':typeof v;
function prepareColumns(data, row){
  let o= {taskID,taskName, start,end,duration, donePercent,after};
  const prow = Object.keys(o);
  if(prow.length !== row.length) throw new Error("wrong size");
  prow.forEach((p,i)=>{data.addColumn(getTyp(row[i]),p);});
}
function drawChart() {
    const data = new google.visualization.DataTable();
    prepareColumns(data, rows[0]);
    data.addRows(rows);
    const chart = new google.visualization.Gantt(googleDiv);
    chart.draw(data, opts);  // opts = {width, height, styles ...}
}
```

And finally, here is the plot of the Gantt chart. The segment lengths are proportional to the duration of each task.

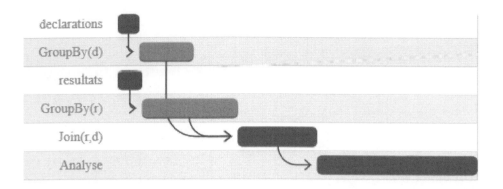

Figure 12.3. *Gantt chart of the six steps in the electoral application*

13

Cartographic Data

13.1. Cartographic application: using cartographic libraries

A cartographic application is of a level of complexity greater than a simple graphic plot, as we have described earlier. We will not try to code it ourselves, even if, for most of the libraries (open source or proprietary), they just draw on a <canvas>. There are various methods for drawing lines or polygons or pixel matrices, for computing topological relations such as sharing a vertex, being included or intersecting each other, and also for computing distances, transforming geographical coordinates between map projections, etc.

It is not our intention to detail any of these numerous features. We will merely present the basic use of one library, open source, which is complete enough to sample all of the most useful features, in a way similar to those of proprietary libraries such as Google, Bing and Yahoo. That library is OpenLayers, code licensed under the "*2-Clause BSD*", with a very active community (2006–2017): at the time of writing this book, the latest version is v4.6.5 (March 18, 2018).

The requirements are the library, the basic styles, and a simple <div> element (or a <canvas>) that will be used by the library:

```
<link rel="stylesheet" href=
"https://cdnjs.cloudflare.com/ajax/libs/openlayers/4.6.4/ol.css">
<body>
<div id="olmap" class="olmap"></div>
<script src=
"https://cdnjs.cloudflare.com/ajax/libs/openlayers/4.6.4/ol.js">
</script>
```

In this application, we use data from four sources:

– a list of French universities, schools of engineering, management, fine arts, etc. as well as large French research institutions, public ones, such as CNRS, Inra, Inria, Inserm, and some private laboratories. Their geographical coordinates are extracted from their Wikipedia pages (they all have one);

– a list of universities from Quebec, the CEGEPS of Quebec and a few laboratories as well. The coordinates have also been extracted from Wikipedia (see section 13.3);

– a list of partnerships between higher education institutions or research laboratories from Quebec and France. Such partnerships can be extracted from lists provided by the universities, from the Federation des CEGEPS and from the lists of joint projects funded by the France-Quebec official partnerships (Samuel de Champlain program, CFQCU, etc.);

– the cartographic source used by the openlayers library: we use OpenStreetMap®, which is *open data* licensed under the Open Data Commons Open Database License (ODbL) by the OpenStreetMap Foundation (OSMF).

The three lists are JSON files. We must make a join, in a way similar to the electoral application, between the list of partnerships and the list of institutions of Quebec (respectively, France). The common key is a normalized label of the institution (the process of normalizing is not described). The first join links the partnerships data with the coordinates of the single point associated with each institution. We can define an *activity index* whose value is the number of partnerships of each institution.

What is really specific in this application is the second join, between the coordinates of the points representing the institutions and the points actually displayed on the canvas by the OpenLayers library. That *cartographic join* allows us to transform the activity of each institution into a marker on the map, displaying that activity: the marker is a circle whose center is the point representing the institution and whose radius is proportional to the activity index.

Here is an example of what we can display on the map of Québec. One similar map can be drawn to display the same activity on the France side.

Higher Education partnerships - Quebec universities

Figure 13.1. *Cartographic application: full display of all data*

In this chapter, we will focus on the *cartographic join*. There are two main operations: the preparation of the map and the display of the markers.

13.1.1. *Preparation of the map*

The sequence of operations to be performed is pretty much the same with every available cartographic library. This code details the sequence with OpenLayers:

```
function prepareMap(latlon, zoom) {
    const sourceUnivs = new ol.source.Vector({});    // empty source
    const layerUnivs = new ol.layer.Vector({ // markers's layer
            title: 'Universities',
            source: sourceUnivs
    });
    const center = ol.proj.fromLonLat([latlon[1],latlon[0]]);
    const map = new ol.Map({
        target: canvasName,
        layers: [new ol.layer.Tile({source: new ol.source.OSM()})],
        view: new ol.View({center, zoom})
    });
    map.on('singleclick', function(e){/* handler: click on map */});
}
```

The construction map object requires several predefined objects:

– target: the drawing surface, the `<canvas>` element in the HTML DOM;

– layers: there is generally one basic layer as the background on top of which to draw other specific layers. The basic layer is the "tiled" version of OpenStreetMaps, referred to as the `ol.source.OSM()`, a given feature of the openlayers library. Moreover, the specific layer for the markers that we will compute later as circles, must be set as an `ol.layer.Vector()` feature: we name it Universities and we attach its source (see below);

– sources: OSM is the first source. The specific Vector layer requires a new source, which we set as `ol.source.Vector({})` and leave empty (`{}`) at first;

– view: the map is a representation of the real world on a flat surface and we need to define which part of the world is to be displayed, using a center location and a zoom factor;

– controls: this is optional. Default values controls the ± signs for interactively modifying the zoom, the scale rule, or other features, which we may optionally modify;

– overlay: an optional special kind of layer which we can use, for instance, with click popups, displaying information linked to a marker.

For short, we can say that, for making a *map*, we need one or several *sources* to be displayed in as many *layers*, transposed within a *view*, displayed onto a *target*, and we can add specific *controls* and display some additional *overlays*.

13.1.2. *Creating a layer of markers*

For each university, we want to compute a marker representing its activity in terms of its number of partnerships. The marker is, a circle, that is, a geometric feature in the vector source, defined by a center and a radius. In the code below, the object `univMark = new ol.Feature({geometry, name, properties})` is that feature, initialized with an `ol.geom.Circle()` geometry, with an identified name, and some additional properties: `{id, np, content}`, which can be used for a popup overlay.

Here is a sample code for the creation of these circles:

```
const fill = new ol.style.Fill({color.'rgba(255,0,0,0.4)'}),
const stroke = new ol.style.Stroke({color:'rgb(0,0,0,1), width:1})
function makeMarker(x, y, np, content, id, fill, stroke) {
  let rad = np * 150 + 2500; // @np: number of partners
  let cen = ol.proj.fromLonLat([y, x]); // @x, @y: point
  const univMark = new ol.Feature({
    "geometry": new ol.geom.Circle(cen, rad, 'XY'),
    "name": id,
    "properties": {id, np, content}
  });
  univMark.setId(id);
  univMark.setStyle(new ol.style.Style({fill, stroke}));
  sourceUnivs.addFeature(univMark);
  return univMark;
}
```

Each marker is pushed into an array and we use its index in that array as its id (used in several places above), which we can relate uniquely to the institution, of which it is the marker. We attach a style (stroke and fill) to each marker. In this case, the style is constant, but it could be computed (e.g. a varying color). The variable content is defined elsewhere.

In Figure 13.1, the markers are created with the full list of partnerships of every institution. It is interesting to allow the user to make a selection, according to one or several filters. After each selection, we start with erasing the previous markers, then we compute the new markers: some universities are filtered out, the radius is recomputed according to the filtered partnerships.

Finally, the map must be "refreshed". Here is the code:

```
const newMarkers = [];        // start with empty
// partnerships: set by JSON reading
// selectedUnivs: from the handler of the selection form
clearMarkers(newMarkers); newMarkers.length = 0;
selectedUnivs.forEach(function(u) { // reset markers
  let np = u.parts.length;
  let content = makePopupToDisplay(u.parts, partnerships);
  newMarkers.push( makeMarker(u.x, u.y, np, content, u.u) );
}
layerUnivs.setMap(map); // refresh the map
```

13.1.3. *Interacting and selecting features*

Here are the results of selecting the partnerships with the interface form on the left: only major topics in engineering or biology are selected. The next map shows the selection over the keyword image (and displays topics on the right).

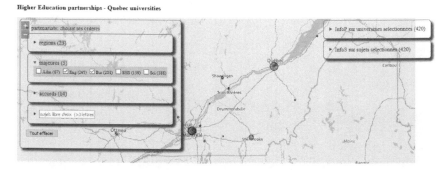

Figure 13.2. *Partnerships selected by major scientific domain*

Figure 13.3. *Partnerships selected by keyword and associated topics*

13.2. SVG-based cartography

We have learnt some bases of the SVG language, which can be:

– autonomous: an SVG document can be directly rendered in a web page;

– embedded: the SVG code can be inserted into an HTML document, providing the associated DTD declaration (xmlns attribute), hence benefiting from DOM access and CSS rules mechanisms.

This application has been used already as illustration in Part 2.

13.2.1. *Description of the application*

Many SVG data are available on the Internet, and especially geographic maps, by country, region or continent. Once selected, the data file can be read by a simple AJAX request, in plain text mode.

We use an SVG file, from WikiMedia commons, of the borders of the countries of the European continent and the Mediterranean rim. It is several megabytes in size, which is voluminous for text data, meant to be processed initially as a string. Therefore, we have first used a preprocessing that degrades gently the precision of the coordinates and the total number of points used for representing the borders. We can easily find online such "svg-optimizers": the result is a 340 kB file.

The main element in that file is the `<path>` element, with its two attributes:

– identifier: `id=number` (supposedly unique);

path descriptor: `d=` `"M83.6619 151.193c-0.2476,0.0627 ...z"`, which generally starts with `M` and ends with `z`, which indicates a polygon in the coordinates that complies with the chosen viewport.

Each country is represented by one `<path>` (simplest case), or several `<path>`, wrapped into a graphic group `<g id=num></g>`, and sometimes nested groups. The United Kingdom is in that most complex category (mainland, NI, Gibraltar and a nested group for islands). Each group can be individually selected. Disputed territories, such as Crimea, or the Golan Heights, are represented that same way.

There is a second source, a JSON file containing information about each country:

```
{
  "countries": [
    {
      "name": "Germany",
      "capitale": "Berlin",
      "EUmember": "1958",
      "money": "euro",
```

```
    "Shengen": "Shengen",
    "population": "81.5",
    "gdp": "3874.5"
  },
  {}
]}
```

The goal is twofold:

– to display the map, therefore, to embed the SVG data into the HTML;

– to access each individual element (path or g), to modify their CSS rules and to use the screen coordinates as a selector of the country information linked to the graphic element. Therefore, the join between the two sources must establish that bidirectional link.

13.2.2. *Embedding the whole SVG document by direct copy*

In Chapter 8, we have described the construction of HTML elements from JavaScript using the "lazy approach". We can do something similar with the SVG document. It is very simple, perfect for the lazy among us (I often use it):

```
<div class="svgExt"><!-- here: the SVG code --></div>
<script>
// const textSVG = ... in the callback of a file request
document.querySelector(".svgExt").innerHTML = textSVG;
</script>
```

the entire SVG text, from <svg> to </svg>, is copied into the <div>; for instance, if the file has been limited to Monaco, we get:

```
<div class="svgExt">
<svg xmlns="http://www.w3.org/2000/svg" viewBox="0 0 230 192.5">
  <g class="maing" transform="translate(-9,-9)">
    <rect x="10" y="10.15" width="228.02" height="189.85">
    <g class="pays memberstate" id="mc">
      <path class="p0" d="M83.6619 151.193c-0.2476,0.0627 -
0.5932,0.1566 -0.9258,0.261510 0 0.0691 -0.4229c0.2099,-0.203
0.4828,-0.1426 0.7337,-0.1075 0.0318,0.0044 0.0933,0.259
0.123,0.268910 0z" />
    </g>
  </g>
</svg></div>
```

13.2.3. *Embedding the SVG code, element by element*

This is the second, *constructive*, approach, where the SVG document is read from file, parsed and each element is added to the HTML DOM, one by one. We must use a special createElement method:

```
const NSuri = "http://www.w3.org/2000/svg"; // namespace svg2000
const svg = document.createElementNS(NSuri, 'svg');
       //     document.createElement('svg') doesn't work
```

There is a namespace specification for every SVG element in svg2000: <g>, <rect>, <path>, etc This constructive approach is not difficult to code but takes more time. However, we can control every step, and add as many appropriate handlers as we may need.

Once the embedding is done, by either approach, the HTML layout engine takes care of the display using CSS rules: it fills in a blue <rect> for the ocean because of: rect {fill:"light blue"}; draws each country with a white background and a black border, because of: path {stroke:"black"; fill:"white"};etc.

13.2.4. *Joining relational data and SVG data*

The identifier chosen for a <g> group representing a country is the standard "a_code", the Internet domain code of that country. Therefore, we need to join that code with the name of the country, as used in the JSON data file. We use a new JSON file for that purpose, containing couples:

```
{"a_code":"de",  "name":"Germany"
{"a_code":"mc",  "name":"Monaco"}
```

The a_code is the value chosen for the id attribute of the <g> elements:

```
<g id="mc"><path class="pays" d=" ... " /></g>
```

We know how to handle such multiple joins.

13.2.5. *Processing the combined information*

Here is a simple example: let us select the countries whose money is the euro. The name of the country is joined with the a code and that a code gives access to the right <g> group. Given the list of these <g>, we can "mark" them, for instance by attributing an additional class name: "euro". Then we can retrieve them and have access to all the concerned <path> elements, and we can change an attribute of their style, for instance the fill color.

```
Array.from(document.querySeletorAll("g.euro"))      // select <g>
.forEach(function(g){
    Array.from(g.querySelectorAll("path"))  // select <path> in g
    .forEach(function(p){p.path.style.fill = 'yellow';});// color
});
```

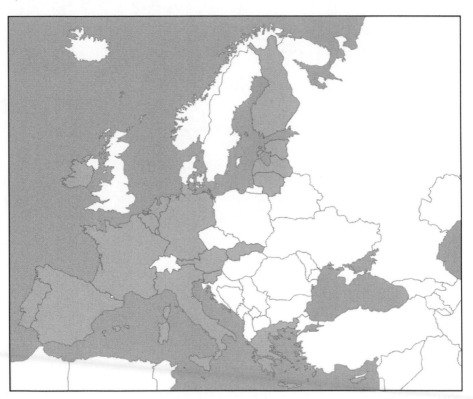

Figure 13.4. *Join between relational and SVG cartographic data*

13.3. Getting coordinates from Wikipedia pages

Here is a very useful feature which we can easily implement: obtaining the coordinates attached to an entry of the Wikipedia encyclopedia.

We can use a direct access to the data through the Wikipedia API[1]:

```
https://en.wikipedia.org/w/api.php?data
```

followed by the appropriate parameters in the data fields:

action=query	the action type;
prop=coordinates	the property to select;
format=json	the ouput format;
titles= ...	name(s) of the page(s) to browse.

For example:

```
https://en.wikipedia.org/w/api.php?action=query&prop=coordinates
&format=json&titles=McGill_University
```

The result is:

```
{"query":{
    "normalized":[{"from":"McGill_University","to":"McGill University"}],
    "pages":{ "7954643":{
        "pageid":7954643, "ns":0,
        "title":"McGill University",
        "coordinates":[{"lat":45.504166,"lon":-73.574722,"globe":"earth"}]
    }}
}}
```

Then we can parse the result, and join the institution's coordinates with extra information on the same institution.

EXERCISE.– use `Fetch` and what you have learned so far, to plot the capital cities of a few European countries (with a radius proportional to population size).

It is possible to group several pages in the same request (pipe sign):

```
https://en.wikipedia.org/w/api.php?action=query&prop=coordinates
&format=json&titles=McGill_University|Université_Laval
```

---

1 https://en.wikipedia.org/w/api.php?action=help&modules=query%2Bcoordinates.

Data Served by JSONP

We know that the "padding" of JSON to JSONP is a workaround to avoid the rule of the *same origin policy*. JSONP was experimented on at the end of 2005 (Bob Ippolito), in order to allow an object literal (JSON format), to be readable as a valid JavaScript code when the script engine is triggered by the tag <script>. This technology is used by some major actors, such as Google, Adobe and Yahoo, but raises some concerns about the risk of "script injection": in other words, the possibility of some malicious code hidden in the data.

Ultimately, the future of JSONP technology seems to be linked to the (commercial) decisions of these giants, but APIs are available today and are of interest wherever a SOP constraint is imposed. Below are three examples of this technology being used.

14.1. Serving RSS feeds through *Yahoo Query Language*

Yahoo proposes a request service whose syntax mimics an SQL command line: it is named *Yahoo Query Language* (YQL). For instance, a YQL request is able to query and send back data from an RSS feed.

This example is made up of two scripts. The first defines the function `rssReturn` which will be used as the *callback wrapper* in JSONP: it reads a selection of the RSS data, such as *title*, *link* and *desc*, and formats a printable answer. The second script is the HTTP request of the JSONP at the Yahoo server, with the YQL syntax: `q=select*..`, `format=json` and `callback=rssReturn` (the same *callback* name).

```
<h1>YQL and RSS: Yahoo serving "ycombinator.com" RSS</h1>
<div class='rss'></div>
<script type='text/javascript'>
function rssReturn(o){
  const rss = (s,t) => s + `<p><a href='${t.link}'>${t.title}</a>
</p> ${t.description}`;
  document.querySelector('.rss').innerHTML =
o.query.results.item.reduce(rss,"");
}
</script>
<!-- The YQL statement will be assigned to src. -->
<script src="https://query.yahooapis.com/v1/public/yql?q=select *
from feed where url='https://news.ycombinator.com/bigrss'
&format=json&diagnostics=true&callback=rssReturn"></script>
```

Two different servers are involved in that application:

– the RSS server: we must know its URL[1] and the JSON data structure (e.g. *title*, *link*, *description*);

– the YQL server: we must know its URL[2] and the request syntax[3]:

```
src ="[url_YQL]? q= [request]
&format=json&callback=rssReturn"
```

and the request itself (beware of not using the same quotes):

```
select * from feed where url='https://news.ycombinator.com/bigrss'
```

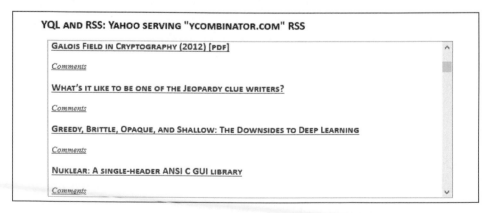

Figure 14.1. *Extracting RSS data as a JSONP served by Yahoo YQL*

---

1 For example, "Hacker news": https://news.ycombinator.com/bigrss.
2 https://query.yahooapis.com/v1/public/yql.
3 https://developer.yahoo.com/yql/guide/yql-tutorials.html.

14.2. Serving shared spreadsheets through Google spreadsheets

There is a popular service in the Google realm which allows any registered user to create and archive tabulated data in a Google-hosted spreadsheet software. The user can also process her/his own data, server side, by using Google Script, which is a Core JavaScript embedded in a Google-side global object.

The Google global object proposes methods for handling the spreadsheet as well as preparing the JSONP. Then, on client side, the user must code the *callback* function, with the same name, to read and process these data.

14.2.1. *Client-side code: HTML and script of the callback function*

As in the previous application, we use two <script> tags, one for defining the *callback* function and one for requesting the JSONP:

```
<h1>Google Spreadsheet Javascript</h1>
 Here are the results of the Presidential election US 2016
<p class='result'></p>
<script>
function callbackFromGS(jp){        //@jp: from JSONP
  document.querySelector(".result").innerHTML =
    jp.data.reduce((s,t)=> s + tr(t), `<table>${tr(jp.head)}`)
    +"</table>";
}
function tr(l){      // for each <tr>, including header
  return l.reduce((s,t)=> s+ `<td>${t.toLocaleString()||""}</td>`,
                  "<tr>") + "</tr>";
}
</script>
<script src="https://script.google.com/macros/s/...[key].../exec?
a1Head=President!A2:J2&a1Data=President!A3:J13&prefix=callbackFrom
GS">
</script>
```

In the JSONP <script>, the "data" part of the URL, after exec?, may contain the limits (using "A1 notation") of the subarray to use, as well as the name of the *callback* function.

Google Spreadsheet Javascript. Here are the results of the Presidential Election US 2016:

State	swing	Clinton	Trump	Others	TEV 2016	Obama	Romney	Others	TEV 2012
Arizona	1	1,161,167	1,252,401	159,597	4,738,332	1,025,232	1,233,654	47,673	4,387,900
Colorado	1	1,338,870	1,202,484	238,866	3,978,892	1,323,102	1,185,243	63,501	3,675,871
Florida	1	4,504,975	4,617,886	297,178	14,601,373	4,237,756	4,163,447	90,972	13,495,057
Iowa	1	653,669	800,983	111,379	2,297,129	822,544	730,617	29,019	2,251,748
Maine	1	357,735	335,593	54,599	1,058,306	401,306	292,276	19,598	1,046,008
Michigan	1	2,268,839	2,279,543	250,902	7,431,589	2,564,569	2,115,256	65,491	7,312,725
Minnesota	1	1,367,716	1,322,951	254,146	3,972,330	1,546,167	1,320,225	70,169	3,861,598
Nevada	1	539,260	512,058	74,067	1,970,426	531,373	463,567	19,978	1,800,969
New Hampshire	1	348,526	345,790	49,842	1,041,147	369,561	329,918	11,493	1,013,420
North Carolina	1	2,189,316	2,362,631	189,617	7,317,507	2,178,391	2,270,395	56,586	6,947,954
Ohio	1	2,394,164	2,841,005	261,318	8,753,269	2,827,709	2,661,437	101,788	8,649,495

Figure 14.2. *Reformatted JSONP data from a Google Spreadsheet request*

14.2.2. *Server-side code under the GoogleScript global object*

The script engine runs in the environment of the GoogleScript global object. For instance, we have access to a `Logger.log` method instead of the more familiar `window.console.log`.

The functions `doGet` and `doPost` are here defined with the same code. The first few lines of `handle` set the selection parameters (possibly a default) and set the *callback*, referred to as `prefix`.

Then come the methods from the GoogleSpreadSheet API[4] which actually read the data and prepare the JSON content before its padding by `prefix()`.

```
function doGet(e){return handle(e)}
function doPost(e){return handle(e)}
function handle(e) {
  const lock = LockService.getDocumentLock(),   // locks access
    a1Head = (e &&e.parameter.a1Head) || "President!A2:J2",
    a1Data = (e &&e.parameter.a1Data) || "President!A3:J53",
    prefix = (e &&e.parameters.prefix) || "callbackFromGS",
    json = {"head": undefined, "data": undefined};
  Logger.log(a1Head +" and "+ a1Data); // simple server test
  try {
    const sps = SpreadsheetApp.getActiveSpreadsheet();
    json.head = sps.getRange(a1Head).getValues()[0];
```

4 https://developers.google.com/apps-script/guides/content#serving_jsonp_in_web_pages.

```
        json.data = sps.getRange(a1Data).getValues();
    }
    catch(e){ json.head = "failure"; json.data = e; }
    finally {      // test: Logger.log(JSON.stringify(json));
        return ContentService
            .createTextOutput(prefix + '(' + JSON.stringify(json) + ')')
            .setMimeType(ContentService.MimeType.JAVASCRIPT);
        lock.releaseLock();
    }
}
```

14.3. Serving images and their metadata through the Flickr API

In this application, somewhat similar to the previous two, we will use a different coding method of sending the JSONP request: the <script> tag will be inserted into the DOM by the first <script>, now alone.

The other difference is that Flickr is both an image repository service and a JSONP service[5], therefore, the same URL hosts the two services.

The application code is as follows. The presentation of results is on a very raw level:

```
const kw = "unicorns";        // you name it
const url = "https://api.flickr.com/services/feeds/";
const photos = "photos_public.gne/?";
const data = "tags=XX&format=json&jsoncallback=jsonpFlickr";
// building the full URI of the service
const urlfull = url+photos+data.replace(/XX/,kw);
window.onload = function(){callWebService(urlfull);}
// callback function
function jsonpFlickr( res ){
    const niv = (x)=>
        Object.values(x).reduce((s,x)=>s+ `${x}, `,"<div>")+"</div>";
    let htm = res.items.reduce((s,x,i)=>
        s+ `<h5>n${i}</h5>${niv(x)}`,"<h2>Flickr and JsonP</h2>");
    document.querySelector(".flickrDiv").innerHTML = htm;
}
// service call: as a JSONP call built on line
function callWebService(url) {
```

---

5 https://www.flickr.com/services/api/flickr.photos.search.html.

```
const script = document.createElement('script');
script.src = url;
document.body.appendChild(script); // triggers the script
}
```

The last line of `callWebService`, which writes the <script> into the DOM, automatically triggers the request to the JSONP. We are sure that the request is sent once the DOM is ready.

Figure 14.3 shows the result of the request.

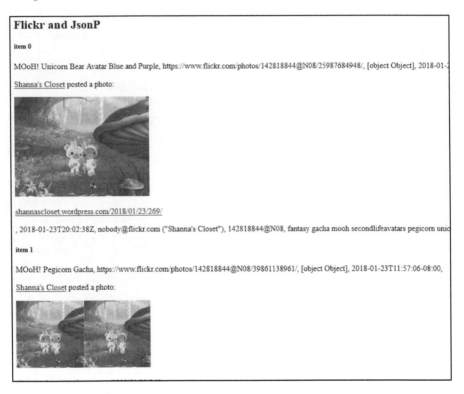

Figure 14.3. *Screenshot: a JSONP request on the Flickr site*

Bibliography

Introduction, general reading

[BRZ 17] BRZUSTOWICZ M., *Data Science with Java: Practical Methods for Scientists and Engineers*, O'Reilly Media, Sebastopol, CA, 2017.

[CRO 14] CROLL A., *If Hemingway Wrote JavaScript*, No Starch Press, San Francisco, 2014.

[DSC 15] DSC, "The free big data sources everyone should know", available at: http://www.datasciencecentral.com/profiles/ blogs/the-free-big-data-sources-every-one-should-know, 2015.

[ICS 16] ICSU, "Open data in a big data world", available at: https://www.icsu.org/ publications/open-data-in-a-big-data-world, 2016.

[NIC 89] NICAR, "Archives", available at: http://ire.org/nicar/, 1989.

[NUS 06] NUSPHERE, "Core JavaScript Reference", available at: http://www. nusphere.com/kb/jscoreref/index.html, 2006.

[VAN 16] VANDERPLAS J., *Python Data Science Handbook: Essential Tools for Working with Data*, O'Reilly Media, Sebastopol, CA, 2016.

Core JavaScript

[BYN 12] BYNENS M., "JavaScript properties", available at: https://mathiasbynens.be/ notes/javascript-properties, 2012.

[COG 11] COGLAN J., "Translation from Haskell to JavaScript", available at: https:// blog.jcoglan.com/2011/03/05/translation-from-haskell-to-javascript-of-selected-portions-of-the-best-introduction-to-monads-ive-ever-read/, 2011.

[CRO 08] CROCKFORD D., *JavaScript: The Good Parts*, O'Reilly Media, Sebastopol, CA, 2008.

[CRO 10a] CROLL A., "Curry: cooking up tastier functions", available at: https://javascriptweblog.wordpress.com/2010/04/05/curry-cooking-up-tastier-functions/, 2010.

[CRO 10b] CROLL A., "Function declarations vs. function expressions", available at: https://javascriptweblog.wordpress.com/2010/07/06/function-declarations-vs-function-expressions/, 2010.

[ELL 11] ELLIOTT E., "Javathcript: Javascript with a lisp", available at: http://kybernetikos.github.io/Javathcript, 2011.

[ELL 14] ELLIOTT E., *Programming JavaScript Applications*, O'Reilly Media, Sebastopol, CA, 2014.

[GRO 12] GROWING WITH THE WEB, "Quicksort", available at: http://www.growingwiththeweb.com/2012/12/algorithm-quicksort.html, 2012.

[JAV 11] JAVASCRIPTKIT, "RegExp (regular expression) object", available at: http://www.javascriptkit.com/jsref/regexp.shtml, 2011.

[MAR 15] MARTENSEN D., "The anatomy of a JavaScript function", available at: https://danmartensen.svbtle.com/the-anatomy-of-a-javascript-function/, 2015.

[MCG 14] MCGANN T., "JavaScript function declarations vs function expressions", available at: http://blog.taylormcgann.com/2014/07/21/javascript-function-declarations-vs-function-expressions, 2014.

[MDN 17a] MDN, "Details of the object model", available at: https://developer.mozilla.org/en-US/docs/Web/JavaScript/Guide/Details_of_the_Object_Model, 2017.

[MDN 17b] MDN, "A re-introduction to JavaScript", available at: http://developer.mozilla.org/en-US/docs/Web/ JavaScript/A_re-introduction_to_JavaScript, 2017.

[OSM 12] OSMANI A., *Learning JavaScript Design Patterns*, O'Reilly Media, Sebastopol, CA, available at: https://addyosmani.com/resources/essentialjsdesignpatterns/book/, 2012.

[PAT 16] PATEL D., "4 JavaScript design patterns you should know", available at: https://scotch.io/bar-talk/4-javascript-design-patterns-you-should-know, 2016.

[PIP 06] PIPONI D., "You could have invented Monads!", available at: http://blog.sigfpe.com/2006/08/you-could-have-invented-monads-and.html, August 2006.

[SIT 16] SitePoint, "Native JavaScript development after Internet Explorer", available at: http://www.sitepoint.com/native-javascript-development-after-internet-explorer, 2016.

[SOS 10] Soshnikov D., "ECMAScript in detail", available at: http://dmitrysoshnikov.com/ecmascript/chapter-7.2-oop-ecmascript-implementation, 2010.

[TRU 13] Truyers K., "JavaScript Namespaces and Modules", available at: https://www.kenneth-truyers.net/2013/04/27/javascript-namespaces-and-modules/, April 2013.

[ZIM 12] Zimmerman J., "JavaScript design patterns: observer", available at: https://www.joezimjs.com/javascript/javascript-design-patterns-observer/, 2012.

JavaScript, Web Client

[HTT 10] Http Archive, "The HTTP Archive tracks how the Web is built", available at: http://httparchive.org, 2010.

[JEN 14] Jenkov J., "SVG tutorial", available at: http://tutorials.jenkov.com/svg/index.html, 2014.

[MIH 17] Mihajlija M., "Building the DOM faster", available at: https://hacks.mozilla.org/2017/09/building-the-dom-faster-speculative-parsing-async-defer-and-preload/, 2017.

[MON 17] MongoDB, "Using MongoDB with Node.js", available at: https://www.mongodb.com/blog/post/the-modern-application-stack-part-2-using-mongodb-with-nodejs, 2017.

[PIL 10] Pilgrim M., "The past, present & future of local storage for web applications", in Pilgrim M., HTML5 Up and Running, O'Reilly Media, Sebastopol, CA, available at: http://diveintohtml5.info/storage.html, August 2010.

[SIM 14] Simpson K., "The basics of ES6 generators", available at: https://davidwalsh.name/es6-generators/, 2014.

[SIM 18] Simplemaps, simplemaps, available at: http://simplemaps.com, 2018.

[SOU 14] Soueidan S., "Understanding SVG coordinate systems and transformations", available at: https://www.sarasoueidan.com/blog/svg-coordinate-systems/, 2014.

[TUT 18] Tutorials Point, "Node.js tutorial", available at: https://www.tutorialspoint.com/nodejs/index.htm, 2018.

Additional reading

[AGU 16] AGUINAGA J., "How it feels to learn JavaScript in 2016", available at: https://hackernoon.com/how-it-feels-to-learn-javascript-in-2016-d3a717dd577f#.2av6msbnj, 2016.

[BER 14] BERNHARDT G., "The birth and death of JavaScript", PyCon'2014, Montreal, Quebec, Canada, available at: https://www.destroyallsoftware.com/talks/the-birth-and-death-of-javascript, 2014.

[BLO 14] BLOOM Z., SCHWARTZ F.S., "You might not need jQuery", available at: http://youmightnotneedjquery.com, 2014.

[JOH 16] JOHNSON P., "Seven reasons JavaScript is better than Java and C++", available at: https://www.youtube.com/watch?v=H0qNUqoJqkQ, 2016.

Index

Other titles from

in

Computer Engineering

2018

ANDRO Mathieu
Digital Libraries and Crowdsourcing
(Digital Tools and Uses Set – Volume 5)

ARNALDI Bruno, GUITTON Pascal, MOREAU Guillaume
Virtual Reality and Augmented Reality: Myths and Realities

HOMAYOUNI S. Mahdi, FONTES Dalila B.M.M.
Metaheuristics for Maritime Operations
(Optimization Heuristics Set – Volume 1)

SEDKAOUI Soraya
Data Analytics and Big Data

SZONIECKY Samuel
Ecosystems Knowledge: Modeling and Analysis Method for Information and Communication
(Digital Tools and Uses Set – Volume 6)

2017

BENMAMMAR Badr
Concurrent, Real-Time and Distributed Programming in Java

HÉLIODORE Frédéric, NAKIB Amir, ISMAIL Boussaad, OUCHRAA Salma,
SCHMITT Laurent
Metaheuristics for Intelligent Electrical Networks
(Metaheuristics Set – Volume 10)

MA Haiping, SIMON Dan
Evolutionary Computation with Biogeography-based Optimization
(Metaheuristics Set – Volume 8)

PÉTROWSKI Alain, BEN-HAMIDA Sana
Evolutionary Algorithms
(Metaheuristics Set – Volume 9)

PAI G A Vijayalakshmi
Metaheuristics for Portfolio Optimization
(Metaheuristics Set – Volume 11)

2016

BLUM Christian, FESTA Paola
Metaheuristics for String Problems in Bio-informatics
(Metaheuristics Set – Volume 6)

DEROUSSI Laurent
Metaheuristics for Logistics
(Metaheuristics Set – Volume 4)

DHAENENS Clarisse and JOURDAN Laetitia
Metaheuristics for Big Data
(Metaheuristics Set – Volume 5)

LABADIE Nacima, PRINS Christian, PRODHON Caroline
Metaheuristics for Vehicle Routing Problems
(Metaheuristics Set – Volume 3)

LEROY Laure
Eyestrain Reduction in Stereoscopy

LUTTON Evelyne, PERROT Nathalie, TONDA Albert
Evolutionary Algorithms for Food Science and Technology
(Metaheuristics Set – Volume 7)

MAGOULÈS Frédéric, ZHAO Hai-Xiang
Data Mining and Machine Learning in Building Energy Analysis

RIGO Michel
Advanced Graph Theory and Combinatorics

2015

BARBIER Franck, RECOUSSINE Jean-Luc
COBOL Software Modernization: From Principles to Implementation with the BLU AGE® Method

CHEN Ken
Performance Evaluation by Simulation and Analysis with Applications to Computer Networks

CLERC Maurice
Guided Randomness in Optimization
(Metaheuristics Set – Volume 1)

DURAND Nicolas, GIANAZZA David, GOTTELAND Jean-Baptiste, ALLIOT Jean-Marc
Metaheuristics for Air Traffic Management
(Metaheuristics Set – Volume 2)

MAGOULÈS Frédéric, ROUX François-Xavier, HOUZEAUX Guillaume
Parallel Scientific Computing

MUNEESAWANG Paisarn, YAMMEN Suchart
Visual Inspection Technology in the Hard Disk Drive Industry

2014

BOULANGER Jean-Louis
Formal Methods Applied to Industrial Complex Systems

BOULANGER Jean-Louis
Formal Methods Applied to Complex Systems:
Implementation of the B Method

GARDI Frédéric, BENOIST Thierry, DARLAY Julien, ESTELLON Bertrand,
MEGEL Romain
Mathematical Programming Solver based on Local Search

KRICHEN Saoussen, CHAOUACHI Jouhaina
Graph-related Optimization and Decision Support Systems

LARRIEU Nicolas, VARET Antoine
Rapid Prototyping of Software for Avionics Systems: Model-oriented
Approaches for Complex Systems Certification

OUSSALAH Mourad Chabane
Software Architecture 1
Software Architecture 2

2013

GHÉDIRA Khaled
Constraint Satisfaction Problems

ROCHANGE Christine, UHRIG Sascha, SAINRAT Pascal
Time-Predictable Architectures

WAHBI Mohamed
Algorithms and Ordering Heuristics for Distributed Constraint Satisfaction Problems

ZELM Martin *et al.*
Enterprise Interoperability

2012

ARBOLEDA Hugo, ROYER Jean-Claude
Model-Driven and Software Product Line Engineering

BLANCHET Gérard, DUPOUY Bertrand
Computer Architecture

BOULANGER Jean-Louis
Industrial Use of Formal Methods: Formal Verification

BOULANGER Jean-Louis
Formal Method: Industrial Use from Model to the Code

CALVARY Gaëlle, DELOT Thierry, SÈDES Florence, TIGLI Jean-Yves
Computer Science and Ambient Intelligence

MAHOUT Vincent
Assembly Language Programming: ARM Cortex-M3 2.0: Organization, Innovation and Territory

MARLET Renaud
Program Specialization

SOTO Maria, SEVAUX Marc, ROSSI André, LAURENT Johann
Memory Allocation Problems in Embedded Systems: Optimization Methods

2011

BICHOT Charles-Edmond, SIARRY Patrick
Graph Partitioning

BOULANGER Jean-Louis
Static Analysis of Software: The Abstract Interpretation

CAFERRA Ricardo
Logic for Computer Science and Artificial Intelligence

HOMES Bernard
Fundamentals of Software Testing

KORDON Fabrice, HADDAD Serge, PAUTET Laurent, PETRUCCI Laure
Distributed Systems: Design and Algorithms

KORDON Fabrice, HADDAD Serge, PAUTET Laurent, PETRUCCI Laure
Models and Analysis in Distributed Systems

LORCA Xavier
Tree-based Graph Partitioning Constraint

TRUCHET Charlotte, ASSAYAG Gerard
Constraint Programming in Music

VICAT-BLANC PRIMET Pascale *et al.*
Computing Networks: From Cluster to Cloud Computing

2010

AUDIBERT Pierre
Mathematics for Informatics and Computer Science

BABAU Jean-Philippe *et al.*
Model Driven Engineering for Distributed Real-Time Embedded Systems 2009

BOULANGER Jean-Louis
Safety of Computer Architectures

MONMARCHE Nicolas *et al.*
Artificial Ants

PANETTO Hervé, BOUDJLIDA Nacer
Interoperability for Enterprise Software and Applications 2010

SIGAUD Olivier *et al.*
Markov Decision Processes in Artificial Intelligence

SOLNON Christine
Ant Colony Optimization and Constraint Programming

AUBRUN Christophe, SIMON Daniel, SONG Ye-Qiong *et al.*
Co-design Approaches for Dependable Networked Control Systems

2009

FOURNIER Jean-Claude
Graph Theory and Applications

GUEDON Jeanpierre
The Mojette Transform / Theory and Applications

JARD Claude, ROUX Olivier
Communicating Embedded Systems / Software and Design

LECOUTRE Christophe
Constraint Networks / Targeting Simplicity for Techniques and Algorithms

2008

BANÂTRE Michel, MARRÓN Pedro José, OLLERO Hannibal, WOLITZ Adam
Cooperating Embedded Systems and Wireless Sensor Networks

MERZ Stephan, NAVET Nicolas
Modeling and Verification of Real-time Systems

PASCHOS Vangelis Th
Combinatorial Optimization and Theoretical Computer Science: Interfaces and Perspectives

WALDNER Jean-Baptiste
Nanocomputers and Swarm Intelligence

2007

BENHAMOU Frédéric, JUSSIEN Narendra, O'SULLIVAN Barry
Trends in Constraint Programming

JUSSIEN Narendra
A TO Z OF SUDOKU

2006

BABAU Jean-Philippe *et al.*
From MDD Concepts to Experiments and Illustrations – DRES 2006

HABRIAS Henri, FRAPPIER Marc
Software Specification Methods

MURAT Cecile, PASCHOS Vangelis Th
Probabilistic Combinatorial Optimization on Graphs

PANETTO Hervé, BOUDJLIDA Nacer
Interoperability for Enterprise Software and Applications 2006 / IFAC-IFIP I-ESA '2006

2005

GÉRARD Sébastien *et al.*
Model Driven Engineering for Distributed Real Time Embedded Systems

PANETTO Hervé
Interoperability of Enterprise Software and Applications 2005

Printed and bound by CPI Group (UK) Ltd, Croydon, CR0 4YY